Mathematical Models in the Social and Biological Sciences

Jones and Bartlett Books in Mathematics

Baum, R.J., *Philosophy and Mathematics*
ISBN 0-86720-514-2

Beltrami, E., *Mathematical Models in the Social and Biological Sciences*
ISBN 0-86720-292-0

Davis, P.J., *Spirals: From Theodorus to Chaos*
ISBN 0-86720-239-4

Eisenbud, D., and Huneke, C., *Free Resolutions in Commutative Algebra and Algebraic Geometry*
ISBN 0-86720-285-8

Epstein, D.B.A., *et al., Word Processing in Groups*
ISBN 0-86720-241-6

Epstein, D.B.A., and Gunn, C., *Supplement to Not Knot*
ISBN 0-86720-297-1

Eves, H., *Fundamentals of Modern Elementary Geometry*
ISBN 0-86720-247-5

Geometry Center, University of Minnesota, *Not Knot* (VHS video)
ISBN 0-86720-240-8

Gleason, A., *Fundamentals of Abstract Analysis*
ISBN 0-86720-209-2

Hansen, V.L., *Geometry in Nature*
ISBN 0-86720-238-6

Harpaz, A., *Relativity Theory: Concepts and Basic Principles*
ISBN 0-86720-220-3

Jones, F., *Lebesgue Integration on Euclidean Space*
ISBN 0-86720-203-3

Loomis, L.H., and Sternberg, S., *Advanced Calculus*
ISBN 0-86720-122-2

Morgan, F., *Riemannian Geometry: A Beginner's Guide*
ISBN 0-86720-242-4

Protter, M.H., and Protter, P.E., *Calculus, Fourth Edition*
ISBN 0-86720-093-6

Redheffer, R., *Differential Equations: Theory and Applications*
ISBN 0-86720-200-9

Redheffer, R., *Introduction to Differential Equations*
ISBN 0-86720-289-0

Ruskai, M.B., *et al., Wavelets and Their Applications*
ISBN 0-86720-225-4

Serre, J.-P., *Topics in Galois Theory*
ISBN 0-86720-210-6

Zwillinger, D., *Handbook of Integration*
ISBN 0-86720-293-9

Mathematical Models in the Social and Biological Sciences

Edward Beltrami

Department of Mathematics
State University of New York at Stony Brook

Jones and Bartlett Publishers
Boston *London*

Editorial, Sales, and Customer Service Offices
Jones and Bartlett Publishers
One Exeter Plaza
Boston, MA 02116

Jones and Bartlett Publishers International
P.O. Box 1498
London W6 7RS
England

Illustrations by Jim Bredt.

Library of Congress Cataloging-in-Publication Data

Beltrami, Edward J.
Mathematical models in the social and biological sciences / Edward Beltrami.
p. cm.
Includes bibiliographical references and index.
ISBN 0-86720-292-0
1. Social sciences—Mathematical models. 2. Biology—Mathematical models. 3. Mathematical models. I. Title.
H61.25B45 1993
300′.1′5118—dc20 92-25309
CIP

Printed in the United States of America

96 95 94 93 92 10 9 8 7 6 5 4 3 2 1

To my mother, Olga Zanellato Beltrami, whose social models were exemplary, if not mathematical.

Contents

Preface

In the early 1960s, a slim volume by John Kemeny and Laurie Snell, *Mathematical Models in the Social Sciences*, caught the imagination of many college-level teachers because it offered novel applications of mathematics in areas other than physics or engineering. That book is now long out of print and, surprisingly, no comparable books have appeared in the interim to fill the gap.

The small book before you is a new upper-level undergraduate text that covers a number of recent applications of calculus-based mathematics to fascinating questions in the social and biological sciences. Our approach is to use materials from research papers that give authentic but accessible applications of mathematical ideas ranging from matrix algebra and Markov chains to intermediate-level probability theory and differential equations. Most of the papers have a nonacademic quality about them, since they draw on familiar experiences and discuss plausible issues. Although some of the material is anecdotal and speculative, the remainder is based on hard empirical evidence. In a few instances, we cite relevant articles from newspapers to give the reader a sense of contact with questions that impact on everyday life.

Mathematical modeling is viewed as an organizing principle that permits one to handle a vast and often confusing array of facts in a parsimonious manner. A good model is a useful metaphor that reveals something of the underlying dynamics. The goal is to gain insight into some complex process, and for this to happen, it is important that a model be fairly simple and transparent, a bit of a caricature perhaps. The models chosen for this book all share these qualities.

The first three chapters deal with issues in the social sciences. The notion of social mobility dominates the first chapter, while the next two are preoccupied with the trade-off between equity and efficiency in government and in the delivery of public services. The fourth and fifth chapters focus on models in ecology and epidemiology in which competition and dispersion play prominent roles. The social sciences intrude even here, however, as we reflect on the interplay between the economics and biology of exploiting natural resources. These considerations reappear in the last chapter, which centers on the idea of competition from a different point of view.

The background required is the usual calculus sequence that includes a bit of matrix theory, some multivariate differential calculus, a brief introduction to differential equations, and an introduction to calculus-based probability. Many junior- and senior-level students in the mathematical sciences have this preparation.

I have included a section in each chapter (except the second, where the techniques are more familiar) that describes the relevant mathematics needed to follow the rest of the chapter. In addition, there are three short appendices that review a few specialized topics. These reviews are admittedly brief and some instructors may wish to expand our treatment, depending on the preparation of the students. I have taught versions of this material in a one-semester junior-senior level class at SUNY at Stony Brook and found that the only stumbling block was the use of differential equations. For this reason, Chapter 4 gives a simpler treatment than the one I used in the classroom, and now only intuitively appealing geometric ideas are employed, augmented by numerically integrated computer graphics generated on a PC. In spite of the simplicity of the means, or perhaps because of it, this suffices to take the student into the core of some fairly demanding models.

A number of colleagues at Stony Brook, past and present, have influenced the development of this book by their work at the interface of mathematics and the other sciences. In particular, I wish to thank Akira Okubo of the Marine Sciences Research Center and Ivan Chase of the Sociology Department for their valuable comments and advice.

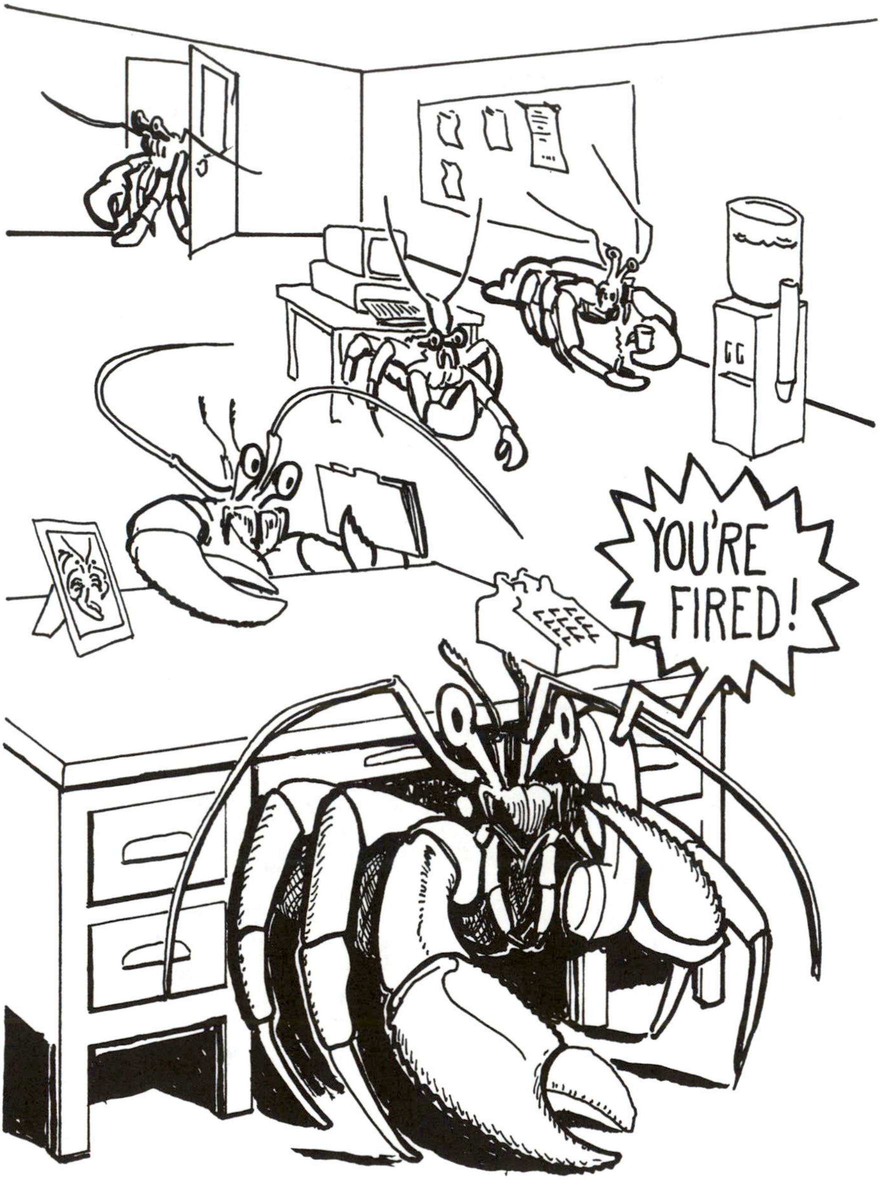
YOU'RE FIRED!

1

Crabs and Criminals

1.1. Background

A hand reaches into the still waters of the shallow lagoon and gently places a shell on the sandy bottom. We watch. A little later, a tiny hermit crab scurries out of a nearby shell and takes possession of the larger one just put in. This sets off a chain reaction in which another crab moves out of its old quarters and scuttles over to the now empty shell of the previous owner. Other crabs do the same until at last some barely habitable shell is abandoned by its occupant for a better shelter, and it remains unused.

One day the president of a corporation decides to retire. After much fanfare and maneuvering within the firm, one of the vice presidents is promoted to the top job. This leaves a vacancy that, after a lapse of a few weeks, is filled by another executive whose position is now occupied by someone else in the corporate hierarchy. Some months pass and the title of the last position to be vacated is merged with some currently held job title and the chain terminates.

A lovely country home is offered by a real estate agency when the owner dies and his widow decides to move into an apartment. An upwardly mobile young professional buys it and moves his family out of the split-level they currently own after selling it to another couple of moderate income. That couple sold their modest house in a less than desirable neighborhood to an entrepreneurial fellow who decides to make some needed repairs and rent it.

What do these examples have in common? In each case, a single vacancy leaves in its wake a chain of opportunities that affect several individuals. One vacancy begets another while individuals move up the social ladder. Implicit here is the assumption that individuals want or need a resource unit (shells, houses, or jobs) that is somehow better (newer, bigger, more status) or, at least, no worse than the one they already possess. There are a limited number of such resources and many applicants. As units trickle down from prestigious to commonplace, individuals move in the opposite direction to fill the opening created in the social hierarchy.

A chain begins when an individual dies or retires or when a housing unit is newly built or a job created. The assumption is that each resource unit is reusable when it becomes available and that the trail of vacancies comes to an end when a unit is merged, destroyed, or abandoned, or because some new individual enters the system from the outside. For example, a rickety shell is abandoned by its last resident, and no other crab in the lagoon claims it, or else a less fortunate hermit crab, one who does not currently have a shell to protect its fragile body, eagerly snatches the last shell.

A mathematical model of movement in a vacancy chainis formulated in the next section and is based on two notions common to all the examples given. The first notion is that the resource units belong to a finite number, usually small, of categories that we refer to as states, and secondly, that transitions take place among states whenever a vacancy is created. The crabs acquire protective shells formerly occupied by snails that have died and these snail shells come in various size categories. These are the states. Similarly, houses belong to varying price/prestige categories, while jobs in a corporate structure can be labeled by different salary/prestige classes.

Let us now consider an apparently different situation. A crime is committed and, in police jargon, the perpetrator is apprehended and brought to justice and sentenced to "serve time" in jail. Some crimes go unsolved, however, and of the criminals that get arrested, only a few go to prison; most go free on probation or because charges are dropped. Moreover, even if a felon is incarcerated, or is released after arrest, or even if he was never caught to begin with, it is quite possible, that the same person will become a recidivist, namely, a repeat offender. What this has in common with the mobility examples given earlier is that here too there are transitions between states, where in this case *state* means the status of an offender as someone who has just committed a crime, or has just been arrested, or has just been jailed, or, finally, has "gone straight" never to repeat a crime again. This, too, is a kind of social mobility and we will see that it fits the same mathematical framework that applies to the other examples.

One of the problems associated with models of social mobility is the difficult chore of obtaining data regarding the frequency of moves between states. If price, for example, measures the state of housing, then what dollar bracket constitutes a single state? Obviously, the narrower we make a price category, the more homogeneous is the housing stock that lies within a given grouping. On the other hand, this homogeneity requires a large number of states, which exacerbates the data gathering effort necessary to estimate the statistics of moves between states.

We chose the crab story to tell because it is a recent and well-documented study that serves as a parable for larger-scale problems in sociology connected with housing and labor. It is not beset by some of the technical issues that crop up in these other areas, such as questions of race that complicate moves within the housing and labor markets. By drastically simplifying the criminal justice system, we are also able to address some significant questions about the chain of moves of career criminals that curiously parallel those of crabs on the sandy sea bottom. These examples are discussed in Sections 1.3 and 1.4.

1.2. Absorbing Markov Chains

We began this chapter with examples of states that describe distinct categories, such as the status of a felon in the criminal justice system

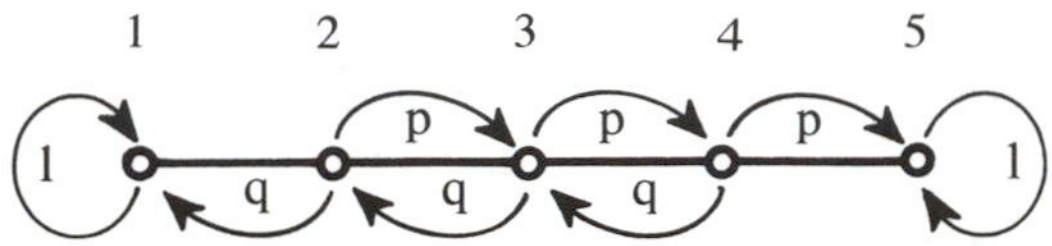

Figure 1.1. Schematic representation of a random walk.

or the sizes of snail shells in a lagoon. Our task now is to formalize this idea mathematically.

The behavior of individual crabs or criminals is largely unpredictable, and so we consider their aggregate behavior by observing many incidents of shell swapping or by examining many crime files in public archives.

Suppose there are N states and that $p_{i,j}$ denotes the observed fraction of all moves from a given state i to all other states j. If a large number of separate moves are followed, the fraction $p_{i,j}$ represents the probability of a transition from i to j. In fact, this is nothing more than the usual empirical definition of probability as a frequency of occurrence of some event. The N-by-N array $\mathbf{P}$ with elements $p_{i,j}$ is called a *transition matrix.*

To give an example, suppose that a particle can move among the integers $1, 2 \dots N$ by bouncing one step at a time either right or left. If the particle is at integer i it goes to $i+1$ with probability p and to $i-1$ with probability $q, p+q=1$, except when i is either 1 or N. At these boundary points, the particle stays put. It follows that the transition probabilities are given by

$$\begin{aligned} p_{i,i+1} &= p \text{ and } p_{i,i-1} = q \text{ for } 2 < i < N-1, \\ p_{1,1} &= p_{N,N} = 1, \text{ and} \\ p_{i,j} &= 0 \text{ for all other } j \,. \end{aligned}$$

The set of transitions from states i to states j is called a *random walk with absorbing barriers* and is illustrated schematically in Fig. 1.1 for the case $N = 5$.

A *Markov chain* (after the Russian mathematician A. Markov) is defined to be a random process in which there is a sequence of moves between N states such that the probability of going to state j in the next step depends only on the current state i and not on the previous history of the process. Moreover, this probability does not depend on when the process is observed. The random walk example is a Markov chain, since the decision to go either right or left from state i is independent of how the particle got to i in the first place, and the probabilities p and q remain the same regardless of when a move takes place.

To put this in more mathematical terms, if X_n is a random variable that describes the state of the system at the nth step then $\text{prob}\,(X_{n+1} = j \mid X_n = i)$, which means "the conditional probability that $X_{n+1} = j$ given that $X_n = i$," is uniquely given by $p_{i,j}$. In effect, a move from i to j is statistically independent from all the moves that led to i and is also independent of the step we happen to stumble on in our observations. Clearly $p_{i,j} \geq 0$ and, since a move from state i to some other state always takes place (if one includes the possibility of remaining in i), then the sum of the elements in the ith row of the matrix P add to 1:

$$\sum_{j=1}^{N} p_{i,j} = 1, \quad 1 \leq i \leq N.$$

The extent to which these conditions for a Markov chain are actually met by crabs or criminals is discussed later. Our task now is to present the mathematics necessary to enable us to handle models of social mobility.

Let $\mathbf{P}^{(n)}$ be the matrix of probabilities $p_{i,j}^{(n)}$ of going from state i to state j in exactly n steps. This is conceptually different from the n-fold matrix product $\mathbf{P}^n = \mathbf{PP}\ldots\mathbf{P}$. Nevertheless, they are equal:

Lemma 1.1. $\mathbf{P}^n = \mathbf{P}^{(n)}$.

Proof. Let $n = 2$. A move from i to j in exactly two steps must pass through some intermediate state k. Since the passages from i to k and then from k to j are independent events (from the way a Markov chain was defined), the probability of going from i to j through k is the product $p_{i,k}p_{k,j}$ (Fig. 1.2). There are N disjoint events, one for

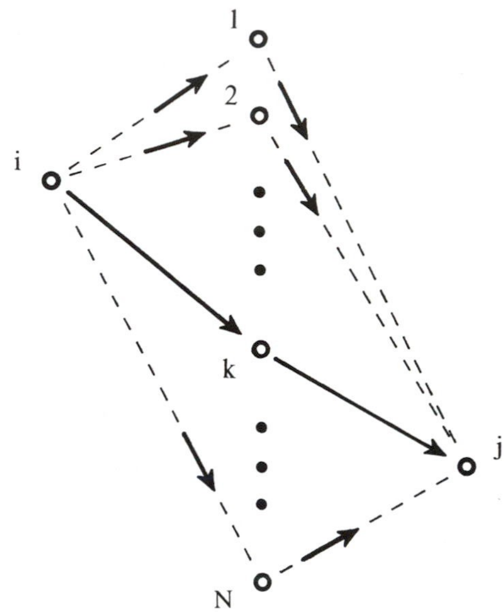

Figure 1.2. Two-step transitions between states i and j through an intermediate state k.

each intermediate state k, and so

$$\sum_{k=1}^{N} p_{i,j}^{(2)} = p_{i,k}p_{k,j},$$

which we recognize as the i,jth element of the matrix product $\mathbf{P}^2$. We now proceed to the general case by induction. Assume Lemma 1.1 is true for $n-1$. Then an identical argument shows that

$$p_{i,j}^{(n)} = \sum_{k=1}^{N} p_{i,k}p_{k,j}^{(n-1)},$$

which is the i,jth element of $\mathbf{P}^n$. □

A state i is called *absorbing* if it is impossible to leave it. This means that $p_{i,i} = 1$. In the random walk example, for instance, the states 1 and N are absorbing.

Two nonabsorbing states are said to communicate if the probability of reaching one from the other in a finite number of steps is positive. Finally, an *absorbing Markov chain* is one in which the first s states are absorbing, the remaining $N - s$ nonabsorbing states all communicate, and the probability of reaching every state $i < s$ in a finite number of steps from each $i' > s$ is positive.

It is convenient to write the transition matrix of an absorbing chain in the following block form:

$$\mathbf{P} = \begin{pmatrix} \mathbf{I} & O \\ \mathbf{R} & \mathbf{Q} \end{pmatrix}, \tag{1.1}$$

where $\mathbf{I}$ is an s-by-s identity matrix corresponding to fixed positions of the s absorbing states, $\mathbf{Q}$ is an $(N-s)$-by-$(N-s)$ matrix that corresponds to moves between the nonabsorbing states, and $\mathbf{R}$ consists of transitions from transient to absorbing states. In the random walk with absorbing barriers and $N = 5$ states (Fig. 1.1), for example, the transition matrix may be written as

$$\mathbf{P} = \begin{array}{c} \\ 1 \\ 5 \\ 2 \\ 3 \\ 4 \end{array} \begin{array}{c} \begin{array}{ccccc} 1 & 5 & 2 & 3 & 4 \end{array} \\ \begin{pmatrix} 1 & 0 & 0 & 0 & 0 \\ 0 & 1 & 0 & 0 & 0 \\ q & 0 & 0 & p & 0 \\ 0 & 0 & q & 0 & p \\ 0 & p & 0 & q & 0 \end{pmatrix} \end{array}.$$

Let f_i be the probability of returning to state i in a finite number of moves given that the process begins there. This is sometimes called the *first return probability.* We say that state i is recurrent or transient if $f_i = 1$ or $f_i < 1$, respectively. The absorbing states in an absorbing chain are clearly recurrent and all others are transient.

The number of returns to state i, including the initial sojourn in i, is denoted by N_i. This is a random variable taking on values $1, 2 \ldots$. The defining properties of a Markov chain assure that each return visit to state i is independent of previous visits and so the probability of exactly m returns is

$$\text{prob}\,(N_i = m) = f_i^{m-1}(1 - f_i). \tag{1.2}$$

The right side of Eq.(1.2) is known as a *geometric distribution* and it describes the probability that a first success occurs at the mth trial of a sequence of independent Bernoulli trials. In our case, "success" means not returning to state i in a finite number of steps. The salient properties of the geometric distribution are discussed in most introductory probability texts and are reviewed in Exercise 1.5.1.

The probability of only a finite number of returns to state i is obtained by summing over the disjoint events $N_i = m$:

$$\begin{aligned} \text{prob}\,(N_i < \infty) &= \sum_{m=1}^{\infty} \text{prob}\,(N_i = m) \\ = \sum_{m=1}^{\infty} f_i^{m-1}(1 - f_i) &= \begin{cases} 0 \text{ if } i \text{ is recurrent} \\ 1 \text{ if } i \text{ is transient} \end{cases} \end{aligned}$$

With probability one, therefore, there are only a finite number of returns to a transient state.

In the study of Markov chains, the leading question is what happens in the long run as the number of transitions increases. The next result answers this for an absorbing chain.

Lemma 1.2. *The probability of eventual absorption in an absorbing Markov chain is one.*

Proof. Each transient state can be visited only a finite number of times, as we have just seen. Therefore, after a sufficiently large number of steps, the process is trapped in an absorbing state. □

The submatrix $\mathbf{Q}$ in Eq.(1.1) is destined to play an important role in what follows. We begin by recording an important property of $\mathbf{Q}$:

Theorem 1.3. *The matrix* $\mathbf{I} - \mathbf{Q}$ *has an inverse.*

Proof. From Lemma 1.1, the elements of the matrix product $\mathbf{Q}^n$ represent the probability of a transition in exactly n steps from some transient state $i > s$ to some other transient state $j > s$. From Lemma 1.2, $\mathbf{Q}^n$ must go to zero as n tends to infinity.

Let $\mathbf{u}$ be an eigenvector of $\mathbf{Q}$ with corresponding eigenvalue λ. It follows immediately that $\mathbf{Q}^n\mathbf{u} = \lambda^n\mathbf{u}$; but, since $\mathbf{u}$ is fixed, the vectors $\mathbf{Q}^n\mathbf{u}$ go to zero as n increases, which implies that λ^n also goes to zero. Hence, $|\lambda| < 1$. This shows that 1 is never an eigenvalue

of $\mathbf{Q}$ or, to put it another way, the determinant of $\mathbf{I}-\mathbf{Q}$ is nonzero.
This is equivalent to the invertibility of $\mathbf{I}-\mathbf{Q}$. □

We turn next to a study of the matrix $(\mathbf{I}-\mathbf{Q})^{-1}$. Our arguments may seem to be a bit abstract, but actually they are only an application of the idea of conditional probability and conditional expectation. A review of the relevant concepts may be found in Appendix A.

Let $t_{i,j}$ be the average number of times that the process finds itself in a transient state j given that it began in some transient state i. If j is different from i, then $t_{i,j}$ is found by computing a conditional mean, reasoning much as in Lemma 1.1. In fact, the passage from i to j is through some intermediate state k. Given that the process moves to k in the first step (with probability $p_{i,k}$), the mean number of times that j is visited beginning in state k is now $t_{k,j}$. The unconditional mean is therefore $p_{i,k}t_{k,j}$ and we need to sum these terms over all transient states, since these correspond to disjoint events (Fig. 1.3):

$$t_{i,j} = p_{i,s+1}t_{s+1,j} + \ldots + p_{i,N}t_{N,j}.$$

In the event that $i = j$, the value of $t_{i,i}$ is increased by one, since the process resides in state i to begin with. Therefore, for all states i and j for which $s < i, j \leq N$,

$$t_{i,j} = \delta_{i,j} + \sum_{k=s+1}^{N} p_{i,k}t_{k,j}, \tag{1.3}$$

where $\delta_{i,j}$ equals 1 if $i = j$, and is zero otherwise. In matrix terms, Eq.(1.3) can be written as $\mathbf{T} = \mathbf{I} + \mathbf{QT}$, where $\mathbf{T}$ is the $(N-s)$-by-$(N-s)$ matrix with entries $t_{i,j}$. It follows that $\mathbf{T} = (\mathbf{I}-\mathbf{Q})^{-1}$.

Let t_i be a random variable that gives the number of steps prior to absorption, starting in state i. The expected value of t_i is

$$E(t_i) = \sum_{j=s+1}^{N} t_{i,j}, \tag{1.4}$$

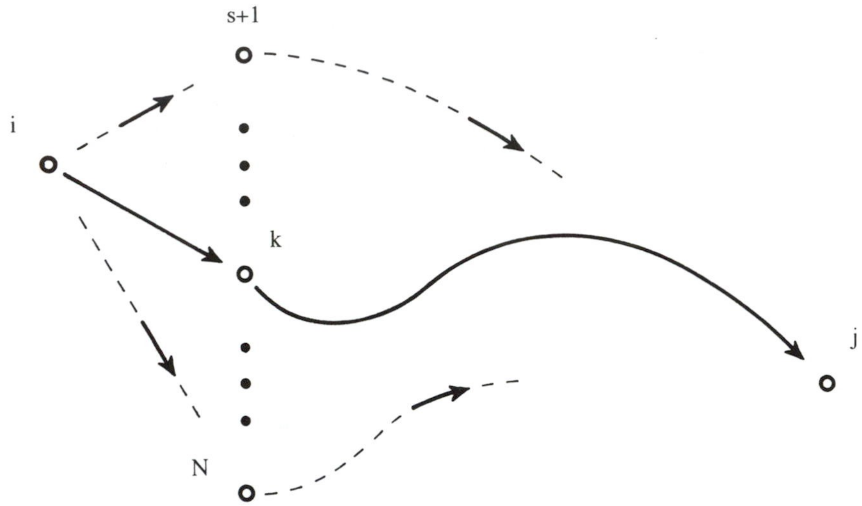

Figure 1.3. Transitions from a state i to state j through some intermediate state k in the first step.

which is the ith component of the vector $\mathbf{Tc}$, where

$$\mathbf{c} = \begin{pmatrix} 1 \\ 1 \\ \cdot \\ \cdot \\ \cdot \\ 1 \end{pmatrix}$$

and $\mathbf{T} = (\mathbf{I} - \mathbf{Q})^{-1}$. Vector $\mathbf{Tc}$ has $(N - s)$ components and the ith one can therefore be interpreted as the average number of steps before absorption when a chain begins in transient state i.

The probability $b_{i,j}$ that absorption occurs in state $j \leq s$, given that it began in some transient state i, can now be computed. Either state j is reached in a single step from i (with probability $p_{i,j}$) or there is first a transition into another transient state k and from there the process is eventually absorbed in j (with probability $b_{k,j}$). The reasoning is similar to that employed earlier; that is, since the moves from i to k and then from k to j are independent by our Markov chain assumptions, we sum over $(N-s)$ disjoint events corresponding to different intermediate states k:

$$b_{i,j} = p_{i,j} + \sum_{k=s+1}^{N} p_{i,k} b_{k,j}, \quad s < i \leq N, \quad j \leq s. \tag{1.5}$$

In matrix terms, Eq.(1.5) becomes $\mathbf{B} = \mathbf{R} + \mathbf{QB}$, where $\mathbf{R}$ and $\mathbf{Q}$ are defined in Eq.(1.1).

Now let $h_{i,j}$ be the probability that a transient state j is ever reached from another transient state i in a finite number of moves. If j differs from i, then evidently

$$t_{i,j} = h_{i,j} t_{j,j},$$

and, since we must add 1 to the count of $t_{i,j}$ when $i = j$, in all cases one obtains

$$t_{i,j} = \delta_{i,j} + h_{i,j} t_{j,j}. \tag{1.6}$$

In matrix terms, this is expressed as $\mathbf{T} = \mathbf{I} + \mathbf{HT}_{\text{diag}}$, where $\mathbf{T}_{\text{diag}}$ is the matrix whose only nonzero elements are the diagonal entries of $\mathbf{T} = (\mathbf{I} - \mathbf{Q})^{-1}$ and $\mathbf{H}$ is the matrix with entries $h_{i,j}$. Therefore, $\mathbf{H} = (\mathbf{T} - \mathbf{I})\mathbf{T}_{\text{diag}}^{-1}$. Note, for later use, that $h_{i,i} = f_i$.

Equations (1.1) through (1.6) will be used in the rest of this chapter.

1.3. Social Mobility

The tiny hermit crab *Pagarus longicarpus* does not possess a hard protective mantle to cover its body, and so it is obliged to find an empty snail shell to carry around as a portable shelter. These empty refuges are scarce and one only becomes available when its occupant dies.

In a recent study of hermit crab movements in a tidal pool off Long Island Sound (see the references to Chase and others in Section 1.6), an empty shell was dropped into the water to initiate a chain of vacancies. This experiment was repeated many times to obtain a sample of more than 500 moves as vacancies flowed from larger to generally smaller shells. A Markov chain model was then

Table 1.1. The number of moves between states in a crab vacancy chain.

From \ To	1	2	3	4	5	6	7	Total Moves
3	0	1	2	7	9	2	0	21
4	0	2	0	3	19	17	1	42
5	4	23	0	2	20	11	10	70
6	6	24	0	0	10	26	26	92
7	2	30	0	0	0	5	22	59

constructed using about half this data to estimate the frequency of transitions between states, with the other half deployed to form empirical estimates of certain quantities, such as average chain length, that could be compared with the theoretical results obtained from the model itself. The complete set of experiments took place over a single season during which the conditions in the lagoon did not alter significantly. Moreover, each vacancy move appeared to occur in a way that disregarded the history of previous moves. This leads us to believe that a Markov chain model is probably justifiable, a belief that is vindicated somewhat by the comparisons between theory and experiment to be given later.

There are seven states in the model. When a crab that is presently without a shelter occupies an empty shell, a vacancy chain terminates, and we label the first state to be a vacancy that is taken by a naked crab. This state is absorbing. If an empty shell is abandoned, in the sense that no crab occupies it during the 45 minutes of observation time, this also corresponds to an absorbing state, which we label as state 2. The remaining five states represent empty shells in different size categories, with state 3 the largest and state 7 the smallest. The largest category consists of shells weighing over 2 grams , the next size class is between 1.2 and 2 grams, and so on, until we reach the smallest group of shells that weigh between .3 and .7 grams. Table 1.1 gives the results of 284 moves, showing how a vacancy migrated from shells of size category i (namely, states $i > 2$) to shells of size j (states $j > 2$) or to an absorbing state $j = 1$ or 2. Thus, for example, a vacancy moved nine times from a shell of the largest size (state 3) to a medium size shell in state 5, while only one of the largest shells was abandoned (absorbing state 2).

Table 1.2. Transition matrix of the crab vacancy chain.

	1	2	3	4	5	6	7
1	1	0	0	0	0	0	0
2	0	1	0	0	0	0	0
3	0	.048	.095	.333	.429	.095	0
4	0	.048	0	.071	.452	.405	.024
5	.057	.329	0	.029	.289	.157	.143
6	.065	.261	0	0	.109	.283	.283
7	.034	.508	0	0	0	.085	.373

Dividing each entry in Table 1.1 by the respective row total gives an estimate for the probability of a one-step transition from state i to state j. This is displayed in Table 1.2 as a matrix in the canonical form of an absorbing Markov Chain (Eq.(1.1)).

We are now in a position to apply the theory of absorbing chains developed earlier in this chapter. The 5-by-5 submatrix in the lower right of Table 1.2 is $\mathbf{Q}$ and $(1-\mathbf{Q})^{-1}$ is easily computed using any of the matrix software packages currently available, or it can be done more painfully by hand. In either case, the result is

$$\mathbf{T} = (\mathbf{1}-\mathbf{Q})^{-1} = \begin{array}{c} \\ 3 \\ 4 \\ 5 \\ 6 \\ 7 \end{array} \begin{array}{c} \begin{array}{ccccc} 3 & 4 & 5 & 6 & 7 \end{array} \\ \begin{pmatrix} 1.105 & .429 & 1.039 & .683 & .562 \\ 0 & 1.102 & .832 & .879 & .629 \\ 0 & .407 & 1.494 & .416 & .530 \\ 0 & .007 & .240 & 1.540 & .750 \\ 0 & 0 & .033 & .209 & 1.697 \end{pmatrix} \end{array},$$

where the entries denote the average number of times $t_{i,j}$ that the process is in transient state j given that it began in transient i. Of interest to us are the components of the vector $\mathbf{Tc}$, where $\mathbf{c}$ is the vector defined previously as having all entries equal to 1. These numbers give the average number of steps required for a vacancy chain to terminate, given that it starts with an empty shell of size i. For example, an average of 3.817 moves take place before absorption whenever an empty shell of the largest size category begins a chain.

Table 1.3 compares averages computed from the model with those obtained empirically through observations, and we see that there is

Table 1.3. Observed and predicted lengths of crab vacancy chains.

Origin state	Observed length	Model computed length
3	3.556	3.817
4	3.323	3.443
5	2.667	2.487
6	2.567	2.538
7		1.939

reasonable agreement. Since no shells of size 7 were put into the water, the last entry in the first column is missing.

Finally, we compute the probability that a vacancy chain terminates in state 1 or 2, given that it begins with a shell of size i. Using Eq.(1.4), this gives us Table 1.4.

For example, starting with a fairly small shell of size 6, the probability that the last shell in a chain remains unoccupied (abandoned) is .861. This high probability reflects the fact that shells that remain at the bottom of the chain are generally cramped and in poor condition, unattractive shelters for all but the most destitute crabs.

Each vacancy is mirrored by a crab moving to a new home except when the last shell is abandoned (absorption in state 2). In this case, the average number of crabs moving to new quarters when a vacancy chain begins in state i is one less than the average vacancy chain length. When a "naked" crab takes the last shell, on the other hand, the average number of crab moves is the same as the average chain length. Conditioning on these two events, we compute the

Table 1.4. Probability that a crab vacancy chain ends in a particular absorbing state.

Origin state	Absorption state 1	Absorption state 2
3	.123	.877
4	.126	.874
5	.130	.870
6	.139	.861
7	.073	.927

average crab mobility M_i in a chain that begins in state i. Simple considerations show that

$$M_i = b_{i,1} + \sum_{j=3}^{7} t_{i,j} - 1. \tag{1.7}$$

(Exercise 1.5.5, where it is shown that the M_i do not compare unfavorably to empirically determined crab mobility averages). Equation (1.7) is of interest because it provides a measure of the accumulated benefit to all crabs in a lagoon resulting from a single commodity becoming available. Since crab size is closely correlated to shell size, those crabs that are able to obtain less cramped shelters tend to grow larger and produce more offspring. The impact of a single vacancy has a multiplier effect as the benefits trickle down to the community of crabs. A similar conclusion would apply in chains initiated by the opening of a new job in some organization or by the sale of a home. For example, all real estate agents benefit from the sale of a single house, since this triggers a bunch of other sales, and the government also benefits by being able to collect multiple sales tax payments.

The averages $t_{i,j}$ give an estimate of the impact that the introduction of a shell of some given size will have on the mobility of crabs and, therefore, on their growth and reproductive capabilities. From Table 1.3, we see that placing a large shell of type 3 into the pool benefits crabs in the intermediate state 5 more than those in state 4. Evidently, the smaller crabs show a preference for a larger than necessary shelter and may delay their reproductive activities until such a unit becomes available. The same conclusion could apply to shrimp, octopuses, and lobsters that take shelter in rock crevices and coral reef openings. Therefore, if the goal is to improve the fitness of these animals, either as a disinterested act of conservation or as a less benign attempt to provide better fishing harvests, then a useful strategy would be to place artificial shelters such as cinder blocks in an appropriate location. The problem is to estimate the benefit that certain creatures would reap from resource units of a certain size. In the case of hermit crabs, at least, the preceding model suggests an answer.

1.4. Recidivism

A felon who commits another crime is said to *recidivate.* Since a criminal is unlikely to confess to a crime unless caught, the true probability of recidivism is unknown. To the police a recidivist is someone who is rearrested, while the correctional system regards a recidivist as someone who returns to jail. There is a need, therefore, to clarify the meaning of these crime statistics, especially since they are often reported in the press and quoted in official reports.

To gain some insight into this problem, a simple Markov chain model is formulated that consists of four states describing the status of an offender as seen by the criminal justice system. The first state corresponds to a former criminal who dies or decides to "go straight" and therefore, one way or the other, does not rejoin the criminal fraternity. This state is absorbing. The remaining states correspond to an individual who has, respectively, just committed a crime, just been arrested, and just been incarcerated (Fig. 1.4).

Let p be the true, but unknown, probability of *recidivism* (a criminal, not caught, commits another crime). We assume that someone who has been arrested and then released has the same propensity p to recidivate as does someone just released from jail. This means, in effect, that the future behavior of a criminal is independent of when he or she returns to society.

From a published paper on the subject (see the references in Section 1.6), the probability p_A of being arrested, given that a crime has just been committed, is estimated to be .25 and, therefore, the unconditional probability of crime repetition is, in this case, $p(1 - p_A) = .75p$. Similarly, the probability p_I of being convicted, sentenced, and institutionalized, given that an arrest just took place, is also estimated to be .25. Hence, the unconditional probability of crime repetition, given that an arrest took place, is $p(1 - p_I) = .75p$. From all transient states $i = 2, 3, 4$, there is also a one-step absorption probability corresponding to someone returning to society as a law-abiding citizen or becoming deceased. Thus, for example, from state 2 just after a crime has been committed, the probability of no recidivism is simply $(1 - p)(1 - p_A)$. This expresses the fact that absorption into state 1 requires two independent events to hold, namely, that no arrest took place after the crime was carried out and

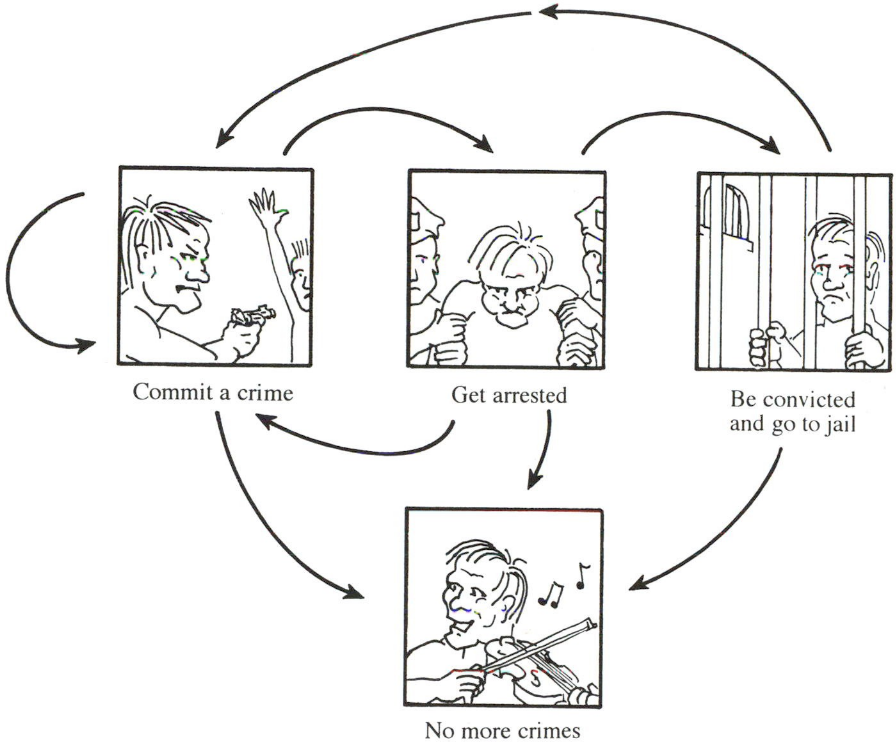

Figure 1.4. Transitions between states in a criminal justice system.

that the offender's criminal career comes to a halt.

Criminal records are prone to errors and are inherently incomplete because they do not include some arrests that may take place outside a local jurisdiction or because a central court file may fail to include arrests for minor offenses. Moreover, some individuals are falsely arrested and convicted, while others are dismissed from prosecution, even if arrested, because the charges are dropped due to insufficient evidence. Nevertheless, we will assume that these blemishes in the data can be disregarded and that the estimated probabilities are essentially correct. Having said this, we can write down the one-step transition matrix as

$$\mathbf{P} = \begin{array}{c} \\ 1 \\ 2 \\ 3 \\ 4 \end{array} \begin{array}{c} \begin{array}{cccc} 1 & 2 & 3 & 4 \end{array} \\ \begin{pmatrix} 1 & 0 & 0 & 0 \\ .75(1-p) & .75p & .25 & 0 \\ .75(1-p) & .75p & 0 & .25 \\ 1-p & p & 0 & 0 \end{pmatrix} \end{array}.$$

The necessary conditions for a Markov chain model are assumed to hold. This means that a move from any state is unaffected by the past criminal history of an individual and that the transition probabilities do not change over time (which is roughly true when these numbers are estimated from data sets spanning a limited number of years).

The matrix $\mathbf{P}$ is in the canonical form in Eq.(1.1) of an absorbing chain in which the block on the lower right is $\mathbf{Q}$. We can compute the 3-by-3 matrix $\mathbf{T} = (\mathbf{I} - \mathbf{Q})^{-1}$ either by hand (simple enough) or by an appropriate computer code to obtain

$$\mathbf{T} = \frac{1}{1-p} \begin{pmatrix} 1 & \frac{1}{4} & \frac{1}{16} \\ p & 1 - \frac{3p}{4} & \frac{1}{4} - \frac{3p}{16} \\ p & \frac{p}{4} & 1 - \frac{15p}{16} \end{pmatrix}.$$

The question of immediate interest to us is the probability of recidivism, given that an individual is in any of the transient states $i = 2, 3, 4$, or, to put it in other terms, the probability of ever returning to transient state i given that it begins there. Since $f_i = h_{i,i}$, we see from Eq.(1.6) that

$$t_{i,i} = f_i t_{i,i} + 1,$$

where f_i is the probability of ever returning to state i in a finite number of steps. Therefore,

$$f_i = 1 - \frac{1}{t_{i,i}}. \tag{1.8}$$

The i,jth component of $\mathbf{T}$ is $t_{i,j}$, and so one need only look at the diagonal components of $\mathbf{T}$ to compute Eq.(1.8). The result is

$$\begin{aligned} f_1 &= p, \\ f_2 &= \frac{p}{4-3p}, \\ f_3 &= \frac{p}{16-15p}. \end{aligned}$$

That f_1 should equal p is not unexpected, since we assumed this to be true initially. Now if $p = .9$, meaning that there is a high likelihood of crime repetition, then the probability f_2 of rearrest is .69, while the probability of re-incarceration f_3 is only .36. The different estimates of recidivism are therefore consistent with each other and simply reflect the fact that separate elements of the criminal justice system (the criminal, the police, and the corrections officer) see crime repetition from different points of view.

From $\mathbf{T}$ it is also seen that the average number of career crimes $t_{2,2}$ is $1/(1-p)$. When $p = .9$, the offender commits an average of 10 crimes during his lifetime, whereas with $p = .8$, there are only five career crimes. Thus, an 11% decrease in the propensity to commit another crime can reduce the number of crimes actually carried out by 50%. This suggests that if increased vigilance on the part of the police has even a small effect in deterring a criminal, this can have a substantial impact on reducing the number of crimes actually committed.

1.5. Exercises

1.5.1. A sequence of statistically independent trials each have two outcomes, success or failure, with probabilities p and $q = 1 - p$, respectively. The random variable X denotes the number of trials until a first success and one sees that prob (X=k) $= q^{k-1}p, \quad k = 1, 2 \ldots$ This is called the *geometric probability distribution.* Show that

$$\sum_{k=1}^{\infty} q^{k-1}p = 1,$$

and that the expected value of X is given by

$$E(X) = \sum_{k=1}^{\infty} kq^{k-1}p = \frac{1}{p}.$$

In Section 1.3, $q = f_i$ and $p = 1 - f_i$. *Hint: What is the sum of a geometric series ?*

1.5.2. Recall the definition of the random variable N_i as the number of times that a Markov chain process is in state i. Using the previous exercise, show that the mean value of this variable is $E(N_i) = 1/(1 - f_i)$. Now let $i = j$ in Eq.(1.6) to conclude that $t_{i,i} = f_i$, a statement that also follows directly from the definitions.

1.5.3. A simplified model of learning in behavioral psychology consists of putting a rat in the maze shown with this exercise in which there are several openings leading into and out of each chamber. If the rat wanders into cubicle 3, it is rewarded by food pellets but a move into the seventh chamber results in an unpleasant shock. Label each of the nine cubicles as a "state." An experimental rat is placed in state 1, for example, and we watch until it reaches state 3 or 7. This is repeated a number of times. If the rat does not learn from his experiences, this is tantamount to supposing that it chooses a doorway at random. That is, if there are k openings available at each step, it selects one of them with probability $1/k$. On the other hand, if the rat learns from his tribulations, then we expect that eventually it will frequently select a pathway that steers away from state 7 and moves towards state 3. One can test this hypothesis by constructing a Markov chain model in which no learning takes place (each doorway is equi-likely) and then comparing the probability of absorption into state 3 as computed from the model with the empirically derived probability obtained from the experiments. Write down the transition matrix for this ab-

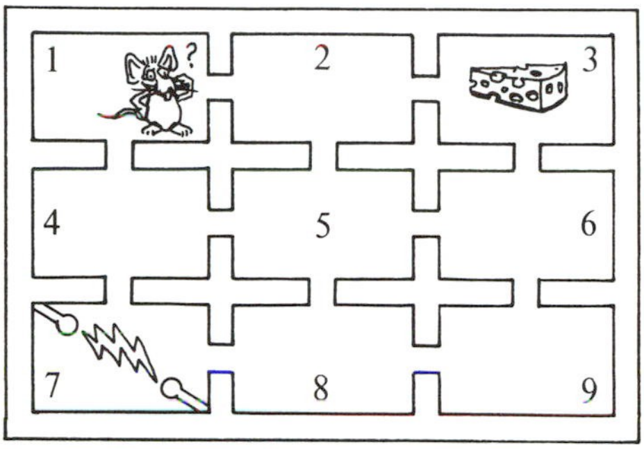

sorbing Markov Chain in the form of Eq.(1.1) and compute the probability that the rat ultimately moves to state 3 given that it begins in state 1. *Hint: Use Eq.(1.5).*

The empirically observed value of being absorbed into state 3 is .95. Would you say, based on the model-computed probability, that the rat has learned to traverse the maze in an advantageous manner?

1.5.4. Consider a random walk model consisting of $N+1$ states $i = 0, 1, \ldots, N$ in which one-step transitions between states take place with the following probabilities:

$$\begin{aligned} p_{i,i+1} &= p, \\ p_{i,i-1} &= 1-p, \qquad \text{for } i = 1.2. \ldots, N-1, \quad \text{and} \\ p_{0,0} &= p_{N,N} = 1. \end{aligned}$$

All other transitions have zero probabilities. This is an absorbing Markov chain, as we saw earlier.

In a later chapter, we will have occasion to show, using a different argument than used so far, that the probability $b_{i,N}$ of absorption in state N, given that the random walk starts in transient state i, is i/N if $p = \frac{1}{2}$. Verify this result using Eq.(1.5) in the case of $N = 4$.

1.5.5. Show that the crab mobility formula of Eq.(1.7) is correct.Compare the average number of crab moves, given that a vacancy begins in state i, with the numbers in the table below obtained empirically from observations:

Origin State	Average number of observed crab moves
3	2.61
4	2.52
5	1.75
6	1.81

1.5.6. Using the model of Section 1.4, with $p = .9$, compute the long-term probability of ever committing a crime again given that an offender has just been arrested. *Hint: Use Eq.(1.6).*

Once again, let $p = .9$ and compute the average number of career jailings for those individuals who have penetrated the criminal justice system far enough to be incarcerated once.

1.5.7. In Eq.(1.4), we saw that the average number of steps $E(t_i)$ to absorption for a chain that begins in state i is the ith component of the vector $\mathbf{Tc}$, where all the entries of column vector $\mathbf{c}$ are equal to 1 and t_i is a random variable giving the number of moves required to be absorbed beginning in i.

There is an alternate derivation of this result. Starting in i, an absorption takes place either in one step, with probability

$$\sum_{j=1}^{s} p_{i,j},$$

or the first step takes us to another transient state k. In this event, the average number of steps prior to absorption is $E(t_k + 1)$, since one move already took place in going from i to k. Therefore,

$$E(t_i) \quad = \quad \sum_{j=1}^{s} p_{i,j} + \sum_{k=s+1}^{N} p_{i,k} E(t_k + 1)$$

$$= \sum_{j=1}^{N} p_{i,j} + \sum_{k=s+1}^{N} p_{i,k}E(t_k).$$

Row sums of the transition matrix $\mathbf{P}$ add to 1, and so this expression may be rewritten in matrix notation as

$$\mathbf{r} = \mathbf{c} + \mathbf{Qr},$$

where $\mathbf{r}$ is the vector with entries $E(t_i)$. We would like to show that $\mathbf{r}$ is the same as $\mathbf{Tc}$; but $\mathbf{Q} = \mathbf{I} - \mathbf{T}^{-1}$ and, therefore,

$$\mathbf{r} = \mathbf{c} + (\mathbf{I} - \mathbf{T}^{-1})\mathbf{r},$$

which verifies that, indeed, $\mathbf{r} = \mathbf{Tc}$.

Essentially, the same argument leads to the variance of t_i. Let $\mathbf{v}$ be the vector with components $\mathrm{Var}(t_i)$. Show that

$$\mathbf{v} = (2\mathbf{T} - \mathbf{I})\mathbf{Tc} - (\mathbf{Tc})^2,$$

where $(\mathbf{Tc})^2$ is the vector whose ith component is the square of $E(t_i)$. Then use this formula to compute $\mathrm{Var}(t_3)$ for the crab vacancy chain problem. *Hint: Recall that* $\mathrm{Var}(t_i) = E(t_i^2) - E^2(t_i)$.

1.5.8. As another example of social mobility, consider a university that has a fixed number of faculty on its staff in four categories or "states": instructor, assistant, associate, and full professors. Each year the teaching staff is evaluated for promotion to the next rank. Let $p_{i,j}$ be the fraction of the staff that moves from rank i to j at the beginning of the academic year, $1 \leq i,\ \ j \leq 4$. If $j = i+1$, this indicates a promotion, while $j = 1$ means no change in rank. If someone in rank i leaves the university, he or she is replaced by an instructor. Thus, there are probabilities p_i, q_i, and h_i for which

$$\begin{aligned} p_{i,i+1} &= p_i, \\ p_{i,i} &= q_i, \\ p_{i,1} &= h_i, \end{aligned}$$

and $p_{i,j} = 0$ otherwise. We assume that $p_i + q_i + h_i = 1$.

Explain why this is a Markov chain and write down the transition matrix $\mathbf{P}$. When is it an absorbing chain?

1.6. Further Readings

A comprehensive treatment of vacancy chains in sociology is in the book by White [1] while the specific model of crab mobility discussed in Section 1.3 is taken from papers [2] and [3] by Chase and others.

While a thorough discussion of recidivism can be found in the book by Maltz [4], the model of Section 1.4 comes from reference [5].

An excellent text on Markov chains, including absorbing chains, with many applications is reference [6]. The same authors also wrote a classic modeling text [7] with applications in the social sciences. Here, too, one finds several Markov chain examples.

2

Congressional Seats and Who Picks Up All the Garbage?

2.1. Background

Most public services are required to meet a weekly demand that varies over time in an uneven manner, often over all seven days of the week and 24 hours a day. The personnel available to match this demand profile must of necessity have overlapping shifts, since no individual expects to work continuously over the week. This is unlike the private sector, in which work requirements are generally uniform with a fixed 9-to-5 workday that coincides exactly with the availability of personnel.

Examples involving public services are not hard to provide. It suffices to mention sanitation workers, policemen, ambulance drivers, nurses in a hospital, security guards, emergency work crews, airport baggage handlers, and transit workers, to name a few. In all these examples, the assignment of workers to different periods of the week is complicated by the fact that the required workload does not match up with the available workforce.

In New York City, for example, there is effectively no refuse collection on Sunday if we exclude certain private carting services. This means that there is even more garbage than usual waiting to be picked up on Monday morning because there is Saturday's backlog to contend with in addition to the trash generated on Sunday. More sanitation men are needed on Monday and, since some refuse, with its attendant smells and hazards, remains uncollected at the end of the day because of the overload, on Tuesday as well. One solution, of course, is to hire additional workers to fill the gap. However, in times of fiscal restraint, this costly solution is unattractive to the municipality that would prefer instead a restructuring of worker schedules to better match the workload. This requires some care, however. Any schedule that consists of irregular and inconvenient work shifts is unsatisfactory to labor. Labor prefers a regular pattern of workdays that gives the employee as many weekends off as possible, for example, or that meets some other "days off" requirement. There is a trade-off here between the needs of the municipality, which would like to get the job done in the face of severe fiscal deficits, and the labor union, which insists on a work schedule that is fair to its members. (The question of salary and benefits is a separate issue that is ignored here.)

In the next section, we discuss a mathematical framework for worker scheduling in the context of an actual labor dispute between the sanitation workers' union and the city of New York that took place some years ago.

A related issue is that of assigning vehicles to carry out a pickup and/or delivery service. This is discussed at length in the next chapter in the context of municipal emergency services, where the vehicles in question are fire engines, ambulances, and the like. For nonemergency vehicle deployment, as in school bus routing or refuse collection, the problems posed are somewhat different. We take a brief look at this in Section 2.4 for the specific situation in which garbage trucks are scheduled for refuse collection so that the cost to a municipality is minimized, while the daily and weekly demand for garbage pickup is satisfied.

Let us switch temporarily to what appears to be a different situation. The United States Constitution stipulates that: "Representatives and direct taxes shall be apportioned among the several states which may be included in this Union, according to their respective numbers..." (Article 1, Section 2). What this says, in effect, is that a fixed number of seats in Congress are to be allocated among the different states so that each state has representation in proportion to its population. This idea of one man–one vote is difficult to meet in practice because the division of seats by population is usually a fraction that must be rounded off. Since political power is rooted in representation, the rounding problem has been a source of controversy and debate throughout the history of the United States, ever since Hamilton, Jefferson, and Adams first struggled to resolve this issue. They, and their successors, attempted to devise a method that would be fair to all states, meaning, among other things, that if a state gains in population after a new census count, then it should not give up a seat to any state that has lost population. We will examine this problem more closely in Section 2.3, where it is seen that what at first glance appears to be a reasonable solution can turn out to violate certain obvious criteria of fairness.

The apportionment problem should remind one of scheduling, in which a designated workload is to be shared by a fixed number of employees so that each worker gets a satisfactory arrangement of days off. Later, in Chapter 3, an analogous question arises in the context of deploying a fixed number of emergency vehicles, such as fire engines, to different sectors of the city so that they can respond effectively to calls for service in a way that is equitable in terms of the workload sustained by each fire company and, at the same time, provides coverage that is fair to all citizens.

In a similar vein is the question of reapportionment, in which a given state with a fixed number of representatives to Congress must now decide to divide the state into political districts. There are a number of ways that a geographical area can be partitioned into sectors of roughly equal population, but partisan rivalry tends to encourage *gerrymandering* in which irregularly shaped districts are formed to favor the election of one candidate over another. In this case, the allocation problem is compromised by considerations that are difficult to quantify.

Evidently, some of these questions are nearly intractable because they are too suffused with political harangues and backroom deals, while others are more susceptible to rational argument. The terms *allocation*, *apportionment*, *assignment*, *deployment* or even *districting* and *partitioning* take on similar meanings, depending on the application, and when a nonpartisan mathematical approach can be sensibly used, it will often come in the form of an optimization problem with integer constraints. This is an approach that is common to a wide number of situations that are only superficially dissimilar, as we will see in this chapter and the next.

2.2. Manpower Scheduling

Before discussing the specific case of New York City sanitation men, let us put the topic of scheduling workers in perspective by looking at another example first. Assume, as is the case in a number of public services, that each employee is assigned to five consecutive days of work followed by two days off. Moreover, if there are several shifts a day, a worker reports for the same time period, such as the 8:00 a.m. to 4:00 p.m. shift. This may not always be true (many urban police departments have rotating eight-hour shifts to cover a 24-hour day), but we limit ourselves to this simple situation, since it already illustrates the basic ideas involved in scheduling.

Suppose that the total workforce is broken into N groups of very nearly equal size. In our case, the only possibilities that exist for days off are Monday–Tuesday or Tuesday–Wednesday or ... Sunday–Monday. Call these feasible periods *recreation schedules* and label them consecutively by the index $i = 1, 2, \dots 7$. Suppose that it has already been determined that in order to meet the average demand, a total of n_i groups must be working on the ith day; that is, $r_i = N - n_i$ groups are permitted that day off. Now let x_j be the number of groups that will be allowed to adopt the jth recreation schedule during any given week. For example, x_3 is the number of times that Wednesday–Thursday is chosen. We would like to develop a schedule so that each group has an identical pattern of days off during an N-week horizon, on a rotating basis. What this means will become more clear as we proceed.

It is apparent that since Tuesday, for example, belongs to the first and second recreation schedule, then $x_1 + x_2$ must equal r_2.

In general, the following system of constraining relations must be satisfied each week:

$$
\begin{array}{ccccccccc}
x_1 & & & & & & +x_7 & = r_1 \\
x_1 & +x_2 & & & & & & = r_2 \\
& x_2 & +x_3 & & & & & = r_3 \\
& & x_3 & +x_4 & & & & = r_4 \\
& & & x_4 & +x_5 & & & = r_5 \\
& & & & x_5 & +x_6 & & = r_6 \\
& & & & & x_6 & +x_7 & = r_7.
\end{array}
\tag{2.1}
$$

This system of equations may be expressed more compactly in matrix notation as $\mathbf{Ax} = \mathbf{r}$ where $\mathbf{A}$ is the matrix given by

$$
\begin{pmatrix}
1 & 0 & 0 & 0 & 0 & 0 & 1 \\
1 & 1 & 0 & 0 & 0 & 0 & 0 \\
0 & 1 & 1 & 0 & 0 & 0 & 0 \\
0 & 0 & 1 & 1 & 0 & 0 & 0 \\
0 & 0 & 0 & 1 & 1 & 0 & 0 \\
0 & 0 & 0 & 0 & 1 & 1 & 0 \\
0 & 0 & 0 & 0 & 0 & 1 & 1
\end{pmatrix}.
$$

Equations (2.1) are readily solvable by elimination. For example, if $r_1 = 1, r_2 = r_5 = 2, r_3 = r_4 = 3, r_6 = 5,$ and $r_7 = 6$, then $N = 11$ and the unique solution is $x_1 = x_5 = 0, x_2 = x_4 = 2, x_3 = x_7 = 1, x_6 = 5$. Thus, the Monday–Tuesday schedule is followed twice, and so forth. Note that since each group gets exactly two days off a week, with N groups one must have

$$\sum_{i=1}^{7} r_i = 2N.$$

Therefore, by adding up equations 2.1, it follows that

$$\sum_{j=1}^{7} x_j = \frac{1}{2}\sum_{i=1}^{7} r_i = N.$$

This means that we can construct a rotating schedule for each group over exactly N weeks. In the example just given in which $N = 11$,

Table 2.1. An 11-week rotating schedule.

	MON	TUES	WED	THURS	FRI	SAT	SUN
1		*	*				
2						*	*
3		*	*				
4						*	*
5			*	*			
6						*	*
7				*	*		
8						*	*
9				*	*		
10						*	*
11	*						*

an 11-week rotating schedule is exhibited in Table 2.1, in which "*" denotes a day off. This chart may be read as either the arrangement of days off for any given group over an 11-week period (each row represents a week) or as a snapshot in any given week of the days in which the 11 different groups are off. (Each row is then one of the groups.) When viewed as an 11-week schedule, it is understood that in the 12th week the schedule repeats itself, starting again from the first row. Also observe that is possible to permute the rows in any fashion. The particular arrangement of Table 2.1 is designed to avoid monotony for the workers by offering a variety of days off. The important factor is that on day i exactly n_i units are working, which is independent of row permutation.

It could happen that the r_i values are different in some other shift, for example, 4:00 p.m. to midnight. In this case, a separate solution is obtained for this period using the same basic argument.

It would appear, therefore, that the matter has been brought to a close. However, there is a hitch. Although Eqs.(2.1) always possesses a unique solution, it may not be an acceptable one. It is essential that the values of x_j be nonnegative and integers, but this is not at all guaranteed. Consider, in fact, the situation in which all $r_i = 1$ except for $r_5 = 2$. Then x_3 turns out to have the value $\frac{1}{2}$, as is easily verified.

It appears that our choice of recreation schedules was too restrictive. To see this, let us augment the set of possible recreation schedules by allowing a single day off in a week. Index Monday only off, Tuesday only off,... by $i = 7, 8, \ldots 14$ and let x_j denote the number of groups that are permitted the jth recreation schedule, as before. Then since Monday, for example, appears on the first, seventh, and eighth recreation schedules, one must have

$$x_1 + x_7 + x_8 = r_1,$$

and, in general, the system (2.1) is replaced by

$$\begin{aligned}
&x_1 \qquad\qquad\qquad\qquad + x_7 + x_8 &&= r_1\\
&x_1 + x_2 \qquad\qquad\qquad\qquad\quad + x_9 &&= r_2\\
&\qquad x_2 + x_3 \qquad\qquad\qquad\qquad\quad + x_{10} &&= r_3\\
&\qquad \vdots\\
&\qquad\qquad\qquad x_6 + x_7 \qquad\qquad\quad + x_{14} &&= r_7.
\end{aligned} \tag{2.2}$$

It is now apparent that a nonnegative integer solution to Eqs.(2.2) always exists. It suffices to set x_i to 0 for $i = 1, 2 \ldots 7$ and then let $x_i + 7 = r_i$. Of course, this is an unsatisfactory solution for the workers who now have only one day off each week. A more acceptable solution would be one in which the number of six-day work weeks is as small as possible. This leads to the problem of minimizing the sum

$$\sum_{j=8}^{14} x_j, \tag{2.3}$$

or, equivalently, of maximizing

$$\sum_{j=1}^{7} x_j,$$

subject to the constraints of Eqs.(2.2) and the condition that the x_j be nonnegative integers. This is the first, but not the last, example that we will encounter in this book of a type of optimization problem known as an *integer program*. Generally, these problems are difficult to solve, but in the present case one can take advantage of the special structure of Eqs.(2.2) to develop a simple algorithm that is suitable for hand computation. We sidestep the details (see, however, Exercise 2.5.1), since our main interest here is another scheduling question.

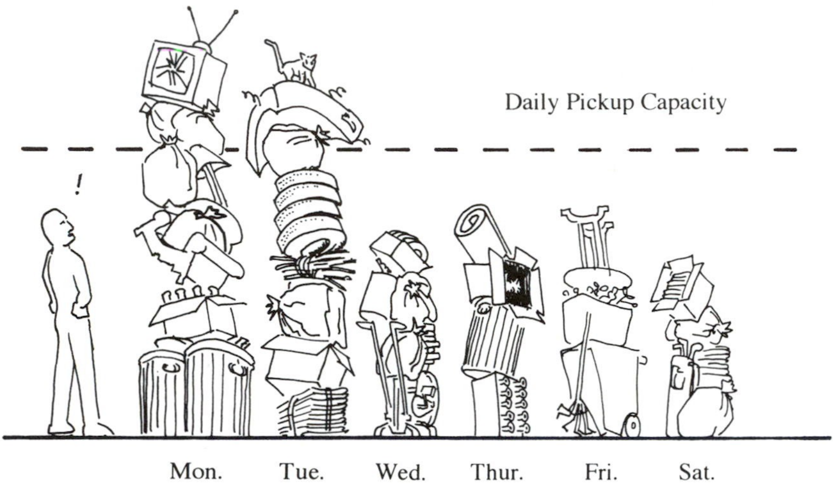

Figure 2.1. The mismatch between workers available and the demand for refuse pickup.

For many years, the sanitation men of New York City worked according to a six-week rotating schedule in which everyone got Sunday off and one-sixth of the workforce had the day off on Monday, another sixth on Tuesday, and so forth. This meant that, Sunday aside, only five-sixths of the workers were available on any given day; but by the 1970s, there was an escalating demand for refuse collection in the city, which translated into a requirement that actually $\frac{14}{15}$ of the pickup crews should have been on the streets on Monday, and nine-tenths on Tuesday, clearly a mismatch between the supply of, and the need for, workers (Fig. 2.1). This discrepancy led the city to negotiate a new labor contract that would solve the problem without having to hire new workers. The story of how this came to pass is told elsewhere (see the references mentioned in Section 2.6), but for us the interesting part is how a revision of the work schedule would accomplish the goal.

A proposal was made to change the existing rotating schedule by dividing the workforce into 30 rather than six equal groups. Recall that $\frac{14}{15}$ of the sanitation crews are needed on Monday. This means that 28 of the $N = 30$ groups should be working on that day, or, using our previous notation, $n_1 = 28$ and $r_1 = N - n_1 = 2$. The remaining days of the week have r values that had been determined to be $r_2 = 3, r_3 = 4, r_4 = 7, r_5 = 7, r_6 = 7$ and, of course, on Sunday $r_7 = 30$.

Guided by the need for integer solutions and mindful of the example worked out earlier in this section, the admissible recreation schedules will include six-day work weeks (only Sunday off) as well as two- and three-day weekends. Let x_i denote the number of times that a Sunday–Monday, Sunday–Tuesday,... Sunday– Saturday schedule is chosen, $i = 1, \dots 6$. A Friday–Saturday–Sunday three-day schedule is chosen x_7 times, while a Sunday–Monday–Tuesday combination occurs x_8 times. Finally, Sunday only is scheduled x_9 times. Labor practices and union regulations stipulate that each worker is to get an average of two days off a week. With $N = r_7 = 30$, this means that

$$\frac{1}{30}\sum_{i=1}^{7} r_i = 2.$$

Since Monday appears on the first and eighth recreation schedules, it follows as before that $x_1 + x_8 = r_1$. Similar relations hold for the other days and we therefore obtain

$$\begin{array}{llllllllll}
x_1 & & & & & & + x_8 & & = r_1 \\
 & x_2 & & & & & + x_8 & & = r_2 \\
 & & x_3 & & & & & & = r_3 \\
 & & & x_4 & & & & & = r_4 \\
 & & & & x_5 & + x_7 & & & = r_5 \\
 & & & & & x_6 + x_7 & & & = r_6 \\
x_1 + x_2 + \dots & & & & & & & x_9 & = r_7.
\end{array} \tag{2.4}$$

Adding the equations in (2.4) shows that

$$2\sum_{j=1}^{8} x_j + x_7 + x_8 + x_9 + \sum_{j=1}^{7} r_j = 2N.$$

From the last row of Eqs.(2.4) and the fact that $r_7 = N = 30$, we obtain

$$\sum_{j=1}^{9} x_j = 30.$$

Taking the last two relations together gives

$$x_7 + x_8 = x_9, \tag{2.5}$$

and therefore, there are just as many six-day workweeks (Sunday only off) as there are weeks with three-day weekends off. At this point, we pause to observe that in the original six-week rotating schedule a Saturday–Sunday–Monday combination would occur naturally every sixth week. The labor union would, of course, prefer to maintain this or some similarly advantageous weekend break under any revised schedule that might be proposed.

Let us begin more modestly by asking for the schedule that gives the largest number of two-day weekends; that is, we want to maximize $x_1 + x_6$ or, equivalently, in view of Eqs.(2.4), to maximize $r_1 + r_6 - x_7 - x_8$. The solution is quite apparent, namely, to let x_7 and x_8 be zero. This gives $x_i = r_i$ for $i = 1, 2 \ldots 6$, with the remaining x_i all zero. The result is then a schedule that provides nine two- day weekends off every 30 weeks. Not bad! The rotating schedule itself is displayed in Table 2.2 and it should be read in the same way as Table 2.1. By suitably permuting the rows in Table 2.2, one can arrange to have seven two-day and two three-day weekends (Exercise 2.5.3), the schedule that was ultimately chosen in the labor negotiations for a new contract with the City of New York.

Returning now to the goal of having as many three-day weekends as possible we see immediately from Eq.(2.5) that there is a price to pay for this luxury, since it would require an equal number of compensatory six-day work weeks. This was not too attractive to the city, since it meant that overtime pay had to be budgeted for the extra day. A compromise solution would have been to trade off two- and three-day weekends and, after much discussion, such a compromise was indeed selected, namely, the one indicated in Exercise 2.5.3.

A more formal approach to choosing a trade-off between two- and three-day weekends can be based on a decision to judge two-day weekends to be "worth" $\frac{2}{3}$ of a three-day weekend. The goal, in this case, is to maximize the weighted sum

$$\frac{2}{3}(x_1 + x_6) + x_7 + x_8. \tag{2.6}$$

Table 2.2. A 30-week rotating schedule.

	Mon	Tues	Wed	Thurs	Fri	Sat	Sun
1						*	*
2		*					*
3		*					*
4		*					*
5	*						*
6			*				*
7			*				*
8	*						*
9			*				*
10			*				*
11						*	*
12				*			*
13				*			*
14						*	*
15				*			*
16				*			*
17				*			*
18						*	*
19				*			*
20				*			*
21						*	*
22					*		*
23					*		*
24						*	*
25					*		*
26					*		*
27					*		*
28						*	*
29					*		*
30					*		*

By Eq.(1.5) this is equivalent to maximizing

$$r_1 + r_6 - \frac{1}{3}(x_1 + x_6).$$

The solution to this problem is left to Exercise 2.5.2, where, as it turns out, only three-day weekends are selected. We can generalize from these examples to place the scheduling problem in a more abstract setting. Suppose that there is a list of M feasible recreation schedules and that the jth schedule is chosen x_j times. Let $a_{i,j} = 1$ if the jth schedule contains day i, and set $a_{i,j} = 0$ otherwise. **A** is the matrix with entries $a_{i,j}$ and we require that $\mathbf{Ax} = \mathbf{r}$, where $\mathbf{r}$ is a vector with components r_i, the given number of groups that can be allowed off on day i, and $\mathbf{x}$ is the vector with components x_j. The problem is to choose the nonnegative integers x_j so as to maximize a weighted sum

$$\sum_{j=1}^{M} c_j x_j,$$

in which c_j are given nonnegative quantities. The two cases considered previously are instances of this integer programming formulation.

2.3. Apportionment

Throughout its rich history, the number of states in our country has increased from the original 13 to the present 50, so that at any moment there were N states, with populations $p_1, p_2, \ldots p_N$. The number of seats in the House of Representatives also grew from an original 65 and at a given moment in history it had a value of h, with h never less than N. The seats are apportioned among the states, with a_i allocated to state i. The sum of the a_i equals h and, of course, the a_i must be integers, with at least one per state. The exact share of h to which the ith state is entitled, its quota q_i, is simply the fraction of h that is proportional to the population of that state, namely

$$q_i = p_i h / \sum_{i=1}^{N} p_i.$$

We have already mentioned the dilemma faced by Congress in allotting these quotas: They need not be integers!

A number of schemes have been devised over the years to mitigate this difficulty. First, note that if some q_i is less than one, then it must be set to unity. Because the House size is fixed at h, the remaining q_i must be adjusted accordingly. This leads us to define a fair share s_i as the largest of the numbers 1 and cq_i, where c is chosen so that the sum of the s_i is now h. For example, if $h = 10$ and $N = 4$, with populations of 580, 268, 102, and 50 (thousand), then the quotas q_i

are 5.80, 2.68, 1.02, and .5. The last state is entitled to one seat and the remaining nine seats are apportioned among the remaining three states, whose quotas are now 5.49, 2.54, and .97. Again, the last state is given exactly one seat, leaving eight to distribute among the other two, whose revised quotas are 5.47 and 2.53. Therefore, $s_1 = 5.47, s_2 = 2.53, s_3 = s_4 = 1$. In 1792, Alexander Hamilton proposed to give the ith state the integer part of s_i, denoted by $[s_i]$, and to allocate the remaining

$$h - \sum_{i=1}^{N} [s_i] = k$$

seats, one each, to the states having the largest remainders. From a mathematical point of view, this amounts to choosing integers $a_i \geq 1$ so as to minimize the sum

$$\sum_{i=1}^{n} (a_i - s_i)^2, \tag{2.7}$$

subject to the condition that

$$\sum_{i=1}^{N} a_i = h, \tag{2.8}$$

which, once again, is an integer programming problem. In effect, it asks for integer allocations a_i that are never less than unity and are as close as possible to the fair shares s_i (which need not be integers), in the sense that they minimize squared difference equation (2.7) while observing constraint Eq.(2.8). This problem admits a simple solution that is identical, as we will see, to Hamilton's proposal. Begin by assigning one seat, the least possible, to each state. Clearly, $1 = a_i \leq s_i$. Next, add one more seat to the state i for which the difference

$$(a_i - s_i)^2 - (a_i + 1 - s_i)^2 = 2(s_i - a_i) - 1 \tag{2.9}$$

is largest. The key idea here is that a_i appears only in the ith term of the sum (2.7) and so Eq.(2.7) is made smallest by allocating the additional unit to the term that most decreases the sum. Continuing in this fashion, we eventually must assign $a_i = [s_i]$ seats to each state. The reason for this is that, as long as $a_i + 1 < s_i$, adding another unit to state i can only contribute to the reduction of Eq.(2.7), and this remains true until a_i is equal to $[s_i]$. Thereafter the remaining k seats are distributed, one each at most, to those states for which, by virtue of Eq.(2.9), the remainder $s_i - [s_i]$ is largest.

Hamilton's idea is, at first sight, a reasonable one, and so it was adopted for a time during the last century. Eventually, however, it was shown to be flawed. This happened after the 1880 census, when the House size increased from 299 to 300. The state of Alabama had a quota of 7.646 at 299 seats and 7.671 at 300 seats, while Texas and Illinois increased their quotas from 9.640 and 18.640 to 9.682 and 18.702, respectively. Alabama had previously been given eight seats of the original 299, but an application of Hamilton's method to $h = 300$ gave Texas and Illinois each an additional representative. Since only one new seat was added, this meant that Alabama was forced to give up one representative for a new total of seven. This paradoxical situation occurred in other cases as well, and it resulted, ultimately, in scrapping Hamilton's idea. What was being violated here is the notion of House monotonicity, which stipulates that, in a fair apportionment, no state should lose a representative if the House size increases.

Thomas Jefferson had a different idea in 1792. He recommended that a_i be the largest of 1 and $[p_i/x]$ where x is a positive number chosen so that the sum of the a_i equal h. As before, $[\cdot]$ means *the greatest integer part of.* The role of x is to be a unique divisor of the population p_i of each state so that representation is determined by the quotient p_i/x. If one state has a greater population than another, its share of House seats is no less than that of the smaller state.

Jefferson's method can be formulated differently. Let S be the subset of all states for which $a_i > 1$. Then, for each i in S,

$$1 < a_i = \frac{p_i}{x} - y_i$$

where $0 < y_i < 1$ is a number that is zero when p_i/x is an integer. By cross-multiplying, it follows that

$$\frac{p_i}{a_i} - \frac{x}{a_i} < x = \frac{p_i}{a_i} - \frac{xy_i}{a_i} \leq \frac{p_i}{a_i};$$

that is, x does not exceed the minimum of p_i/a_i over all i in S. From the left side of the inequality, we obtain $x > p_i/(a_i+1)$. When $[p_i/x] \leq 1$, then $a_i = 1$ and so $p_i/x < a_i + 1$. In all cases then, x is greater than the largest of $p_i/(a_i+1)$. Putting all this together gives

$$\max \frac{p_i}{a_i+1}\bigg|_{\text{all } i} < x \leq \min \frac{p_i}{a_i}\bigg|_{i \text{ in } S}, \tag{2.10}$$

where min, max are shorthand, respectively, for *minimum of* and *maximum of*. Conversely, if Eq.(2.10) is satisfied, then the right side of the inequality shows that $1 < a_i \leq p_i/x$ for each i in S, while the left side of Eq.(2.10) gives us $a_i + 1 > p_i/x$ for all i. Therefore, $a_i = [p_i/x]$ for all i in S; otherwise, $a_i + 1 \leq p_i/x$, which is a contradiction.

However, when Jefferson's method was applied to the 1792 census in which $h = 105$, an anomaly occurred in which Virginia's fair share of 18.310 was rewarded with 19 seats while Delaware's share of 1.613 gave it only one seat. The larger state was favored over the smaller one, an imbalance that was frequently observed using Jefferson's method from 1792 to 1840, during which there were five censuses. John Quincy Adams proposed a modification of the procedure in which $[\cdot]$ now meant *rounding up to the next largest integer*; but this tended to favor smaller states at the expense of the larger ones. Daniel Webster suggested a compromise in 1832 in which $[\cdot]$ was to mean that *one rounds off to the nearest integer*. By an argument similar to the one given earlier, Webster's method implies the existence of an x for which

$$\max \frac{p_i}{(a_i+1/2)} \leq x \leq \min \frac{p_i}{(a_i-1/2)} \tag{2.11}$$

(Exercise 2.5.5), and it seemed to give results more reasonable than either of the methods proposed by Jefferson or Adams. Indeed, as Balinski and Young argue in their thorough discussion of the problem (in a book referenced in Section 2.6), Webster's method goes a long way towards satisfying a bunch of fairness criteria, including the previously mentioned House monotonicity requirement. Interestingly, Webster's approach, which was adopted for only a decade beginning in 1840, also satisfies an integer program. To show this, we observe first that the per capita representation of state i is a_i/p_i, while the ideal per capita representation, across all states of the union, is h/p, where p is the combined population of all states together. Consider now the sum of the squared differences of a_i/p_i to h/p weighted by the population of state i:

$$\sum_{i=1}^{N} p_i \left(\frac{a_i}{p_i} - \frac{h}{p} \right)^2 = \sum_{i=1}^{N} \frac{{a_i}^2}{p_i} - \frac{h}{p}. \tag{2.12}$$

Choosing integers $a_i \geq 1$ to minimize Eq.(2.12) subject, of course, to their sum being equal to h, we get Webster's method. In fact, since h^2/p is constant, we see from Eq.(2.12) that it suffices to minimize the sum of the ${a_i}^2/p_i$. If an optimal choice has been made, then interchanging a single seat between two states r and s cannot reduce Eq.(2.12) when $a_r > 1$. Keeping the allocations to all other states the same, the interchange implies that

$$\frac{(a_r - 1)^2}{p_r} + \frac{(a_s + 1)^2}{p_s} \geq \frac{{a_r}^2}{p_r} + \frac{{a_s}^2}{p_s},$$

or,

$$\frac{p_r}{(a_r - 1/2)} \geq \frac{p_s}{(a_s + 1/2)}. \tag{2.13}$$

We claim that

$$\min \frac{p_i}{(a_i - 1/2)} < \max \frac{p_s}{(a_s + 1/2)},$$

for otherwise there exist integers r and s for which Eq.(2.13) is violated. Condition (2.11) is therefore satisfied.

Although mathematical convenience often dictates the choice of an objective function in a minimization problem, the previous examples should dispel the idea that this can be done with impunity. The decision of what function to optimize needs to be examined carefully in terms of the intended application. Another example of this ambiguity will appear in the next chapter.

We close by touching on the reapportionment problem mentioned at the beginning of this chapter, in which a state with k representatives must now partition its geographical area into political districts. Even more than the apportionment issue, the question of districting is rooted in a struggle for power, since it directly affects the ability of a candidate to be elected to Congress. The ethnic and racial makeup of a neighborhood can favor one political party over another, and the way district boundaries are drawn affect the balance of votes. Nevertheless, one can at least pose some aspect of the problem mathematically and, even if it is somewhat artificial, the formulation is useful in terms of applications to more benign problems of partitioning a region into service areas such as school districts, postal zones, and police precincts.

Suppose that the state is divided into N parcels of land — census tracts, to be specific — and that we wish to form k contiguous districts from these parcels to correspond to k seats in the House of Representatives. Imagine, by looking at a map of the state, that a number M clusters of the N parcels have been formed, generally overlapping, that constitute potential political districts. The procedure for actually carrying out this partitioning is a separate matter that can itself be formalized, but we bypass this step here, much as we skipped the question of how feasible "recreation schedules" were formed in the Manpower Scheduling problem. The only requirement in forming the M clusters is that they be feasible in terms of being reasonably compact in size and not too misshapen (not too "gerrymandered"), as well as connected (no enclaves).

Let $a_{i,j} = 1$ if tract i belongs to the jth feasible cluster and $a_{i,j} = 0$ otherwise, and let $x_j = 1$ if the jth cluster is to be actually chosen as one of the political districts, with $x_j = 0$ otherwise. The population of tract i is p_i and so the total population of cluster j is

$$p(j) = \sum_{i=1}^{n} a_{i,j} p_j.$$

If p is the state's total population, then the population of each district should ideally be p/k to achieve equal representation. In effect, $p(j)$ should differ from p/k as little as possible. This leads to the integer program of minimizing the sum of squared differences

$$\sum_{j=1}^{M} x_j (p(j) - p/k)^2,$$

subject to the constraint

$$\sum_{j=1}^{M} x_j = k,$$

which ensures that exactly k districts are formed out of the M potential ones. Whether this formulation has any merit in practice is arguable, but at least it poses the problem in a coherent and parsimonious manner and helps us to recognize the possible connections to similar districting problems.

2.4. Vehicle Scheduling

A city has a fleet of large trucks that pick up refuse at selected nonresidential sites, such as schools, hospitals, and other public buildings, where there are trash bins that are hoisted onto the truck by forklift and then compacted. When the trucks fill up, they go to a disposal site to empty their loads and then they return to pick up more refuse at other locations. In this way, they make a number of back-and-forth trips that can be linked together to form a daily schedule for a single truck, provided that the total time does not exceed the time allotted for a single work shift (a workday of six to eight hours). The concatenation of several back-and-forth tours to a dump to form a daily route that satisfies the time constraint is called a *feasible truck schedule.* Implicit in this is that each tour requires less time to complete than the time available in a shift, in conformity with the usual situation in which time is the binding constraint in forming daily routes out of tours, whereas vehicle capacity is the limiting factor in the formation of the tours themselves. Generally, more than one vehicle is required to satisfy all the clients in one day, and so one wants to form schedules that require the least number of trucks.

Suppose that a large number M of such feasible truck schedules have been put together from the separate round trip tours that cover all the clients, at a total of N locations. This is usually done by "eyeballing" a street map of the region being serviced, although more sophisticated techniques are available to do this that are not considered here. There may be considerable overlap among the M schedules, since there are several ways of hooking together round trips to the dump without exceeding the time constraint.

Since we want a selection of schedules that uses the least number of trucks, this can be posed as an optimization problem. In the spirit of the districting problem of the preceding section, let $a_{i,j} = 1$ if the ith client belongs to the jth schedule, with $a_{i,j} = 0$ otherwise. Also, let $x_j = 1$ if schedule j is selected, with $x_j = 0$ otherwise. Then one wishes to minimize the sum

$$\sum_{j=1}^{M} x_j,$$

subject to the condition that each pickup point lies on some route or other:

$$\sum_{j=1}^{m} a_{i,j} x_j \geq 1$$

for $i = 1, 2 \ldots N$. The last equality ensures that all N pickup points are serviced.

A somewhat different set of scheduling problems arise from the fact that in practice not all sites are serviced the same number of times each week. Up to now, we assumed that the daily and weekly schedules for a truck are the same, but in some areas the clients have their refuse removed on Monday, Wednesday, and Friday (MWF), others on Tuesday, Thursday, and Saturday (TTS), while the remainder are serviced every day (except Sunday). In this context, the formation of a weekly schedule is uncoupled from that of finding daily schedules. If one assumes that three-times-a-week customers are indifferent to whether they get an MWF or TTS schedule, the problem is to assign tours to days of the week so as to minimize the number of required vehicles. Rather than treat this problem directly, we focus instead on the subtle question of whether weekly schedules can be formed at all.

We begin by collecting a bunch of round trip tours to the dump, much as before, except that we label them as either *red* or *green* tours, corresponding to MWF or TTS. The only proviso is that six-times-a-week pickup points must appear on both a green and red tour if they are to be serviced once every day but Sunday, and not

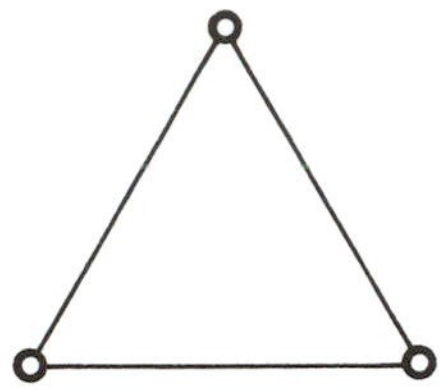

Figure 2.2. A tour graph that is not two-colorable.

twice on the same three days of the week. However, there may be a difficulty here. To see how this can arise, let us form a *tour graph* in which the vertices denote tours, and an edge is inserted between two vertices whenever the corresponding tours have a six-day-a-week point in common. Recall that a graph G is a set of points called *vertices* that are joined by line segments called *edges*.

The six-times-a-week sites are to appear on exactly two tours having distictly different colors, and so adjacent vertices in the tour graph must be painted differently. That this cannot always be done is shown by the graph in Fig. 2.2, where we see that the service frequency requirement is violated. In this case, the set of tours is infeasible. In general, the least number of colors necessary to paint the vertices of any graph so that no adjacent vertex has the same color is called the *chromatic number* of the graph. The following result tells us when a tour graph has chromatic number 2:

Lemma 2.1. *A tour graph is two-colorable if and only if it has no cycles of odd order.*

Proof. Suppose that the graph has no odd-order cycles. This means that a traversal from a given vertex along edges of the graph back to itself to form a closed loop involves only an even number of edges. Pick any such vertex and paint it with one of the two colors; for example, red. Then touch all the vertices adjacent to it with green paint. Repeat this until all vertices are painted. In this way, no vertex is ever painted with both colors, since this can only happen when there are two paths between two vertices, one of the paths having an even number of edges and the other odd; but this

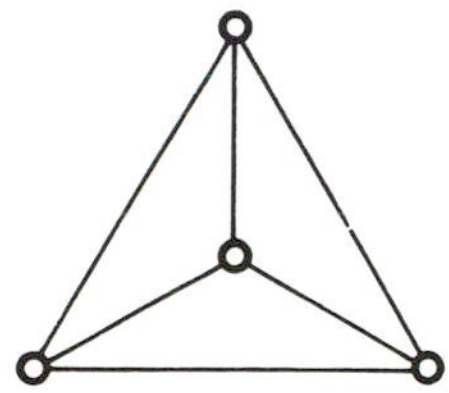

Figure 2.3. A tour graph that is not three-colorable.

implies a circuit of odd length, a contradiction. Conversely, when a graph can be colored with only two colors, then the pigments must alternate when a cycle is traversed. Hence, the length of such a cycle must be even. □

It is apparent that the trouble with the graph depicted in Fig. 2.1 is that it consists of a single cycle of odd length. In general, the same difficulty can arise with other service frequency requirements. Consider, for example, sites that are serviced Monday–Thursday (MW), Tuesday–Friday (TF), Wednesday–Saturday (WS), or every day of the work week. In this case, the round trip tours are painted with three colors for the three different service frequencies, with six-times-a-week points to appear exactly once on a tour of each type to guarantee that they be serviced once every day of the week and not several times on some subset of the days.

Form a tour graph as before, with an edge between vertices if the tours have a six-day point in common, and label all vertices as either red, green, or blue. It is apparent that the service frequency requirement can be met in a feasible manner only if the tour graph can be painted with the three colors in such a way that adjacent vertices have different pigments; that is, we want the graph to have a chromatic number of 3. Figure 2.3 shows that in general this cannot be done.

A question of interest is to determine the chromatic number of a graph. To do this, one defines an *independent set* in a graph to be a subset of vertices such that no two of them are adjacent. Index all maximally independent independent sets by $j = 1, 2 \ldots M$, and label them by I_j. Let $a_{i,j} = 1$ if vertex i belongs to I_j, with zero otherwise,

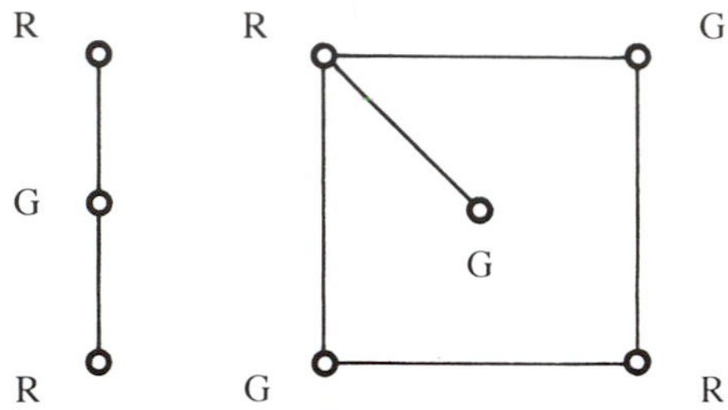

Figure 2.4. A tour graph with different tour assignments.

and let $x_j = 1$ if subset I_j is chosen, with zero otherwise. Then one wishes to minimize the number of independent sets that are required to cover the graph completely. Some of the I_j may overlap, of course. The mathematical formulation of this optimization problem is left to Exercise 2.5.7, and its solution tells us whether the collection of given tours is feasible in terms of satisfying the service frequency. With multiple service frequencies, the problem of finding the least number of garbage trucks is now more complicated. Assuming that a feasible coloring exists, one needs to form daily routes that pick up all points on MWF or TTS, for example, while satisfying the time constraint. Consider, for example, the tour graph shown in Fig. 2.4. The graph is not connected, since there is no *apriori* reason why round trip tours must share the same six-times-a-week point in common. Because there are no circuits of odd length, Lemma 2.1 tells us that it can be two-colored. There are evidently four ways of coloring the graph, one of which is indicated in the figure. Assuming that each truck can cover only two tours a day, the assignment of red or green can make the difference between needing two trucks every day or three on alternate days, and so the task of finding the least number of vehicles must now take the choice of coloring into consideration. However, this will not be pursued further.

2.5. Exercises

2.5.1. An algorithm for minimizing Eqs. (2.3) subject to the constraining relations (2.2) is not hard to implement. From Eqs. (2.2), we observe that

$$x_j = r_j - x_{j+7} - x_{j-1} \leq r_j - x_{j-1},$$

in which x_0 is set equal to x_7 and $j = 1, 2 \ldots 7$. The same relations also show that

$$x_j \leq r_{j+1}$$

for all j. Now define

$$x_j = \min(r_j - x_{j-1}, r_{j+1}), \tag{2.14}$$

in which r_8 is set equal to r_1. The last equation in (2.2) shows that

$$x_7 \leq \min(r_1, r_7), \tag{2.15}$$

and so it follows that x_j are nonnegative for all j. The algorithm begins by choosing an initial value of x_0, namely, x_7, in relation (2.14), to compute x_1. From Eq.(2.15), there are only a finite number of choices. Since x_j takes on the largest possible value for each $j = 1, 2 \ldots 7$, it suffices to apply Eq.(2.14) for each initial choice of x_0 and compute the corresponding sum of the x_j to obtain the largest possible sum. The same choice also minimizes Eq.(2.3) because Eq.(2.14) always picks the value $r_j - x_{j-1}$ (unless constrained to choose the smaller value r_{j+1}), and this then forces x_{j+7} to be zero. Otherwise, x_{j+7} is nonnegative. (Show this !)

Try this procedure for the case in which $r_1 = 5$, $r_2 = r_5 = 2$, $r_3 = 6$, $r_4 = r_6 = 3$, and $r_7 = 1$. We see that x_0 is either zero or one, and so there are two possible solutions to the integer program.

2.5.2. Find the maximum of the weighted sum (2.6) subject to the constraints (2.4) to obtain a solution to the sanitation problem. Recall that $r_1 = 2$, $r_2 = 3$, $r_3 = 4$, $r_4 = r_5 = r_6 = 7$, $r_7 = 30$. Show that the solution is the same as maximizing the number of three-day weekends and write down a 30 week rotating schedule for any given worker. Show that $x_9 = 9$.

Note that we seek integer solutions x_j that are non-negative. Show, for arbitrary choices of the r_i, that the largest number of three-day weekends, namely, the maximum of $x_7 + x_8$, is given by

$$\min(r_1, r_2) + \min(r_5, r_6).$$

2.5.3. By permuting rows in Table 2.2, show that it is possible to arrange for two three-day weekends and seven two-day weekends, without requiring six-day work weeks.

2.5.4. Complete the formulation of the integer programming problem of finding the chromatic number of a graph, as discussed in Section 2.4.

2.5.5. Establish the inequalities (2.11) that define Webster's apportionment method. *Hint: Employ reasoning similar to that used in deriving Eq.(2.10) in the text.*

2.5.6. Suppose that N customers share a public facility, such as a reservoir. The cost of the service must be allocated fairly among the users by a system of fees. This is a topic that is not unrelated to the apportionment problem and it has a number of ramifications. (See, for example, the book *Cost Allocation* edited by P. Young, Elsevier North-Holland Press, 1985.) We touch on only one aspect here.

Let S be a subset of the N users and $C(S)$ the least cost of servicing all the customers in S most efficiently. If S is empty, then the cost is zero. Moreover, if x_i is the fee charged to the ith customer, we impose the break-even requirement that

$$\sum_{i=1}^{N} x_i = C(N).$$

Since the N customers are cooperating in the venture of maintaining the utility, it seems reasonable that no participant or group of participants should be charged more than the cost required to provide the service:

$$\sum_{i \text{ in } S} x_i \leq C(S). \tag{2.16}$$

A related idea is that no participant or subset of participants should be charged less than the incremental cost of including them in the service. Since the incremental cost is $C(N) - C(N-S)$, one requires that

$$\sum_{i \text{ in } S} x_i \geq C(N) - C(N-S). \tag{2.17}$$

Inequality (2.16) expresses the incentive for voluntary cooperation among the participants, while Eq.(2.17) is a statement of equity, since a violation of this inequality by some subset S of users means that S is being subsidized by the remaining $N - S$ customers. In effect, these inequalities express the idea that the individuals have formed a coalition to share both costs and benefits fairly. Show that Eqs.(2.16) and (2.17) are equivalent.

2.5.7. A single day is broken down into six work shifts for the police department in a certain town in order to cover manpower requirements which vary at different times (see table).

Each member of the police force works a consecutive eight-hour period, and so only four feasible work clusters exist that satisfy this requirement, as one readily verifies from the table. Let $a_{i,j} = 1$ if the ith shift appears on

Shift	Police Required on Duty
midnight–2 a.m.	6
2 a.m.-8 a.m.	4
8 a.m.-noon	5
noon-4 p.m.	6
4 p.m.-6 p.m.	8
6 p.m.-midnight	10

the jth work period of eight hours duration, with $a_{i,j} = 0$ otherwise. Define x_j to be 1 if the jth work period is chosen and zero otherwise. Formulate and solve the integer programming problem of minimizing the number of police officers needed each day subject to the condition that the ith shift is to appear on some eight-hour period or other at least n_i times, where n_i is the number of police required on duty during the ith shift, as given in the preceding table. If each person works exactly five days a week, what should the total work force be to cover an entire work week ?

2.6. Further Readings

The revised New York City Sanitation Department work schedules were agreed on in a new contract in 1971 and, according to the *New York Times* ("City wants to redeploy sanitation men for efficiency," Feb.11, 1971, and "Sanitation union wins $1,710 raise in 27 month pact," Nov. 17, 1971), "city officials described the new pact as a major breakthrough in labor relations in the city because salary increases were linked to specific provisions to increase productivity." The complete story is told in the paper by Mechling[8]. A mathematical reference to Manpower Scheduling can be found in [9].

The apportionment problem for the U.S. Congress is captivatingly discussed in the book by Balinski and Young [10]. One of the pitfalls of modeling optimization questions was revealed in Section 2.3, in which we saw that a formal minimum provided little or no guidance in resolving the underlying issue of fairness.

The reapportionment, or political districting, problem is illustrated by the troubled experience of California, which had gained seven new seats in the last census to give it a total delegation of 52 members to Congress in 1992 ("California is torn by political wars over 7 new seats," *New York Times*, March 3, 1991).

Vehicle routing is treated in papers [11] and [12] which are based, in part, on experiences in advising the New York City Sanitation Department.

S&L
POLICE
RESCUE
TRAFFIC CONTROL

3

While the City Burns

3.1. Background

What began as a flare-up on the kitchen stove quickly spreads to the wood counter and smoke fills the room. An alert homeowner calls the emergency fire department number; within minutes, a fire engine company, siren blaring, shrieks to a halt in front of the apartment and the blaze is soon under control. Scenes like this are enacted daily in cities and towns all over the country and are familiar enough; but sometimes the consequences are more dire and there can be considerable loss of life and property. To reduce, if not entirely eliminate, these losses is the primary mission of a fire department, whose size and operation must be adequate to match the level of service required by the public. Insurance codes and municipal regulations stipulate a minimum of coverage, to be sure, but during periods of escalating demand, especially in inner city ghettos, the number of incidents stretch the available resources. City budget cutbacks and fiscal belt tightening make it less probable that more firefighting equipment and personnel can be added to the existing departmental roster, and it forces the chief and his or her aides to rethink the deployment of the forces currently at their disposal to make them more effective. Although we focus here on fire services, the same predicament faces virtually all public emergency services, including ambulance, police, and repairs.

The number of fire companies and their geographic distribution affect the ability to respond to an alarm in a timely manner, but it is difficult to assess by just how much. A doubling of fire companies is likely to reduce response time, for example, but the magnitude of effect is arguable. Nevertheless, *response time*, namely, the time from when an alarm is called in to the moment that the first fire company arrives at the incident, remains a useful proxy measure of how a redeployment of firefighting units can reduce property losses and fatalities. This leads to the problem of how to allocate fire companies to different portions of a city so as to minimize response time, given that the total number of firefighting units is fixed. This is considered in Sections 3.3 and 3.4.

Two kinds of units are typically involved, an engine company whose pumper truck hooks up to a fire hydrant to deliver water, and a ladder company that does rescue work by breaking into a burning building. Similar considerations apply to both, and we will not distinguish between them.

Alarm rates fluctuate throughout the day, and they also vary considerably from high-density areas in the urban core to the more sparsely populated regions at the edge of the city. Moreover, during peak alarm periods, often in late afternoon and evening, some fire companies could be busy and consequently not available to respond immediately to a new alarm. The time a unit is busy, from the moment of its initial dispatch until it is again available for reassignment, is also somewhat unpredictable. For these reasons, the deployment problems will be modeled in terms of random variables, and the mathematics needed is reviewed in the next section.

Fire companies are placed in firehouses (sometimes more than one to a house) that are located in sectors of the city where fires are expected to occur. Shifting demographics over the years have rendered some of these locations to be less favorably positioned than they were intended to be originally, but by and large, more companies are located in high-demand areas such as the central business district and less, for example, in residential areas. However, a residential area may contain high-risk fire hazards, such as schools, and its residents are penalized for low incidence rates by more dispersed fire companies and, therefore, greater response times. This inequity in coverage can be adjusted by shifting some of the units in high-alarm areas to the residential zones, but this creates an imbalance in the workload of the firefighting units, since each responds to more calls than those in the more sparsely populated part of town. We therefore see that there are several, possibly conflicting, "fairness" criteria that are reminiscent of the multiple objectives encountered in the previous chapters in different guises. The trade-off between these goals is discussed again in Section 3.4 together with other deployment issues. The analysis of these problems is based on work done by the Rand Institute in New York City more then two decades ago. (See the references in Section 3.6.)

3.2. Poisson Processes

A sequence of events occur randomly in time and we count the number $N(t)$ that have taken place up to time t. With an eye towards the applications later in this chapter, we think of $N(t)$ as the number of fire alarms that arrive at some central dispatcher (either by phone or through fire alarm call boxes) by time t. $N(t)$ is a nonnegative and integer-valued random variable that satisfies the relation $N(s) \leq N(t)$ for $s < t$, with $N(0) = 0$.

We assume that the number of calls that arrive in disjoint time intervals are statistically independent. This assumption is called *independent increments* and may not be quite true for fire alarms, since a call that is not answered immediately could allow a minor flare-up to escalate into a serious fire that would trigger a flurry of other calls over a span of time. Nevertheless, it seems to be a reasonable hypothesis most of the time.

We also assume that the probability distribution of the number of arrivals that take place in any time interval depends only on the length of that interval and not on when it begins. In other words, the number of calls in the interval $(t_1 + s, t_2 + s)$, namely, $N(t_1 + s)$-$N(t_2 + s)$, is distributed in the same way as the number of calls that take place in (t_1, t_2), namely, $N(t_1) - N(t_2)$, for all $t_1 < t_2$ and $s > 0$. This condition, called *stationary increments*, is violated for fire alarms, since the frequency of fires varies with the time of day. However, one can reconcile this hypothesis with real data by restricting our observations to peak alarm periods, when the arrival rate of calls is fairly constant.

Let us now define a *Poisson process* (after the French mathematician S. Poisson) to be a counting process with stationary and independent increments for which the probability distribution of the random variable $N(t)$ is

$$\text{prob}\,(N(t) = k) = (\lambda t)^k e^{-\lambda t}/k! \tag{3.1}$$

for $k = 0, 1, \ldots$ The constant λ is called the *rate* of the process for reasons to become clear in a moment. Note that by the stationary increments requirement, we have $\text{prob}\,(N(t+s) - N(s) = k) = \text{prob}\,(N(t) = k)$.

Let $o(t)$ denote terms in t of second or higher order. These are negligible terms when t is small enough. From Eq.(3.1), we obtain

$$\text{prob}\,(N(t) = 1) = \lambda t e^{-\lambda t} = \lambda t(1 - \lambda t + (\lambda t)^2/2 - \ldots) = \lambda t + o(t),$$

and, in a similar manner,

$$\text{prob}\,(N(t) \geq 2) = 1 - \text{prob}\,(N(t) = 0, 1) = o(t).$$

These relations show that if t is small enough, the probability of more than one arrival in an interval of duration t is negligible and the probability of a single arrival is roughly equal to λt.

The expected value of $N(t)$ is easily computed to be λt (Exercise 3.5.1), which permits us to interpret λ as the average number of events per unit time. This, and a number of other facts about the Poisson distribution, can be found in any number of books on stochastic processes (see, for example, the reference to the book by Ross in Section 3.6) or are left as exercises.

When m Poisson processes are taking place simultaneously and independently, it is not unreasonable that the sum is also Poisson:

Lemma 3.1. *Let $N_i(t)$ be independent Poisson random variables at rates λ_i, for $i = 1, 2, \ldots m$. Then the sum $N(t) = N_1(t) + N_2(t) + \ldots N_m(t)$ is also Poisson at rate $\lambda = \lambda_1 + \lambda_2 + \ldots \lambda_m$.*

Proof. Begin with the case $m = 2$. Since the event $N(t) = k$ occurs in $k + 1$ disjoint ways, namely, $N_1(t) = i$ and $N_2(t) = k - i$, for $i = 0, 1, \dots k$, we can sum over the $k + 1$ events to obtain

$$\operatorname{prob}(N(t) = k) = \sum_{i=0}^{k} \operatorname{prob}(N_1(t) = i, N_2(t) = k - i)$$

(see Appendix A). Moreover, the separate counting processes are statistically independent, and so the last sum becomes

$$\begin{aligned} \sum_{i=0}^{k} \frac{(\lambda_1 t)^i e^{\lambda_1 t} (\lambda_2 t)^{k-i} e^{\lambda_2 t}}{i!(k-i)!} &= \frac{t^k e^{-(\lambda_1+\lambda_2)t}}{k!} \sum_{i=0}^{k} \frac{k!(\lambda_1)^i (\lambda_2)^{k-i}}{i!(k-1)!} \\ &= t^k (\lambda_1 + \lambda_2)^k e^{-(\lambda_1+\lambda_2)t} / k!, \end{aligned}$$

using the binomial theorem. Now proceed by induction. If the sum of the first $m - 1$ processes is already Poisson, then all we need do is to add the last one to this sum, which is again the case of two Poisson processes considered earlier. □

A continous random variable T is said to be *exponentially distributed* at *rate* μ if

$$\begin{aligned} \operatorname{prob}(T \leq t) &= 1 - e^{-\mu t}, \quad t \geq 0, \\ &= 0, \qquad\qquad t < 0. \end{aligned} \tag{3.2}$$

The expected value of T is readily verified to be $1/\mu$ (Exercise 3.5.1).

Let $T_1, T_2, \dots$ denote the length of time between successive events of a Poisson process. A little thought shows that

$$\sum_{i=1}^{k} T_i \leq t \quad \text{if and only if} \quad N(t) \geq k. \tag{3.3}$$

In the special case of $k = 1$, we therefore see that

$$\operatorname{prob}(T_1 \leq t) = 1 - e^{-\mu t},$$

and so T_1 is exponentially distributed.

It is true in general, moreover, that the T_i are independent and identically distributed exponential random variables. This result is not proven here, since it is used only incidently shortly, although it is not really difficult to do. (See, for example, Chapter 5 of the book by Ross referenced in Section 3.6.) Because of this fact, there is no need to use subscripts to indicate which gap is being considered, and T will denote the interval between any two arrivals.

Suppose that one begins to observe a Poisson process at some random time $s > 0$, and then wait until the first call arrives. The time gap between two successive arrivals is interrupted, so to speak, by the sudden appearance of an observer. It is a remarkable fact that the duration of time until the next event as seen by the observer has the same exponential distribution as the gap length of the uninterrupted interval. This is called the *memoryless property*, since it implies that the past history of the process has no effect on its future. In more mathematical terms, this is expressed by saying that the conditional probability of a gap length T greater than $t + s$, given that no call took place up to time s, is the same as the unconditional probability of a gap exceeding t:

$$\text{prob}\,(T > t + s \,|\, T > s) = \text{prob}\,(T > s), \text{ for all } s, t > 0. \qquad (3.4)$$

Using the definition of conditional probability (see Appendix A for a review), Eq.(3.4) is equivalent to

$$\text{prob}\,\frac{(T > t + s, T > t)}{\text{prob}\ \ (T > t)} = \text{prob}\,(T > s),$$

or, to put it another way,

$$\text{prob}\,(T > t + s) = \text{prob}\,(T > t)\,\text{prob}\,(T > s).$$

The last identity is certainly satisfied when T is exponentially distributed.

Suppose there are two concurrent and independent Poisson processes. A patient observer will see the next arrival from either the first or the second process. The probability that the next occurrence is actually from process $i, 1 \leq i \leq 2$, is λ_i/λ, where λ is the sum $\lambda_1 + \lambda_2$. We prove this in terms of the inter-arrival times T and T' of two simultaneous Poisson processes:

Lemma 3.2. *Let T and T' be independent and exponentially distributed random variables at rates μ_1 and μ_2. These define the inter-arrival times from two Poisson processes at rates μ_1 and μ_2. The* *probability that the first arrival occurs from the process having rate i is μ_i/μ, where μ is the sum of μ_1 and μ_2.*

Proof. Let $i = 1$. A similar argument then applies to $i = 2$. We need to compute prob $(T < T')$. The density function of the variable T' is $\mu_2 e^{-\mu_2 t}$, and so by conditioning on the variable T' (see Appendix A), we obtain

$$\text{prob}\,(T < T') = \int_0^\infty \text{prob}\,(T < T' \mid T' = s)\mu_2 e^{-\mu_2 s} ds.$$

However, since T and T' are independent, the last integral becomes

$$\int_0^\infty \text{prob}\,(T < s)\mu_2 e^{-\mu_2 s} ds = \int_0^\infty (1 - e^{-\mu_1 s})\mu_2 e^{-\mu_2 s} ds = \mu_1/\mu.$$

□

The time from when an alarm is received by a dispatcher until a fire company arrives at the incident and completes its firefighting operations is called the *service time*. We assume that the successive service times of a particular fire company define a Poisson process in which the kth "arrival" occurs when the kth service is complete, ignoring idle periods during which the company is not working. From now on, we use the more appropriate term *departure*, since our concern is with completion of service, and the preceding discussion shows that consecutive departure times are independent exponential random variables. Service times of a fire company are in fact not exponentially distributed in general, but the results obtained by making this assumption give results that are reasonably close to those obtained in practice, as will be seen later.

The fire companies operate more or less independently, and if m of them are busy at incidents, this constitutes m independent and identically distributed Poisson processes at rates μ (that is, average service times $1/\mu$). From Lemma 3.1, their combined rate is $m\mu$, and so the average time required for some company or other to become the first to complete its service is then $1/m\mu$. If a new alarm arrives from a Poisson process at rate λ while the m units are busy, then in view of the memoryless property of the exponential, the service time remaining from the receipt of the call is again exponential at a mean rate of $1/m\mu$.

Now suppose that a municipality has a total of N fire companies and that they all are busy. The arrival of a new alarm at rate λ is unconnected with the departure of a call presently in service, and so we have two independent and concurrent Poisson processes at rates λ and $N\mu$. Lemma 3.2 now shows that the probability that the new call must wait for a busy unit to become available (namely, that an arrival occurs before a departure) is $\lambda/(\lambda + N\mu)$.

Imagine that the peak alarm period has been going on for some time so that incoming calls and service completions have reached a sort of equilibrium in which the average number of alarms that arrive equals the average number of departures. In this case, it is evident that if the average number of busy units is M, then $M\mu$ is the average departure rate from the system. Since this equals the mean arrival rate λ, we obtain the relation

$$M = \lambda/\mu. \tag{3.5}$$

The formula (3.5) is well known in queueing theory, which is the mathematical study of waiting lines, and can be established rigorously under a fairly general hypothesis. We will need to apply Eq.(3.5) in the next Section.

A spatial Poisson process is defined in a way similar to a temporal process. Suppose events take place in the plane at random and that if S is any subset of the plane, then $N(S)$ counts the number of events that occur within S. If S and S' are disjoint subsets, then we require that $N(S)$ and $N(S')$ be independent random variables (*independent increments*) and that $N(S)$ depend only on the area of S and not on its position or shape (*stationary increments*). When E is the empty set, then $N(E) = 0$.

The spatial counting process is called Poisson if

$$\text{prob}\,(N(S) = k) = (\gamma A(S))^k e^{-\gamma A(S)}/k!,$$

where $k = 0, 1, \ldots$ and $A(S)$ is the area of S. The rate constant γ is easily shown to be the average number of events per unit area, using an argument analogous to that employed in the temporal case.

It is useful to know how to estimate the rate constant λ in a Poisson process. Break a time interval t into n small pieces of size h, so that $t = nh$, and count how many arrivals actually occur during

t. Call this m. By independent increments, what happens in a given interval is independent of whether or not an arrival occurs in any other interval. The probability of an arrival in an interval of length h is one minus the probability of no arrival, which, by the Poisson distribution, is roughly λh, as we saw earlier, with the approximation getting better as h tends to zero for fixed t, or equivalently, as t gets larger when h is fixed. Moreover, the probability of more than one arrival during h is roughly zero, for the same reason. Therefore, we have a sequence of independent trials with two outcomes, arrival and non-arrival (*Bernoulli trials*), and so the the average number of arrivals during t is $n\lambda h$. It follows that

$$m = n\lambda h = \lambda t \quad \text{or} \quad \lambda = \frac{m}{t}, \text{ for large enough } t.$$

For spatial processes the same result holds in the form $\gamma = m/A(S)$ for planar regions S of sufficiently large area.

3.3. The Inverse Square Root Law

A large region S of area $A(S)$ has N firehouses scattered at random according to a spatial Poisson distribution at rate γ. The rate constant is the average number of firehouses per unit area and, according to our previous discussion, is estimated to be $N/A(S)$. Alarms arrive as a Poisson process at rate λ and any fire company that is dispatched remains busy for a length of time that is exponentially distributed with a mean duration of $1/\mu$. We assume one fire company per house, a requirement that is modified later, and that calls arrive during peak alarm periods during which the mean λ can be considered to be constant. The more quiet periods of the day, if there are any, are less interesting, since the demand for service can be satisfied more readily.

An incident occurs somewhere at random, uniformly distributed within S, and the closest available unit is dispatched. Implicit here is that alarms are just as likely to happen in one part of the region as another. This implies that S is fairly homogeneous in terms of hazards, as would be the case in a number of residential areas. For the moment, it is also assumed that all N units are available, a restriction that will be relaxed later to account for the fact that some fire companies may be busy at other alarms.

Let us think of S as a portion of a metropolis in which the street network is a grid of crisscrossing intersections. This means that travel to an incident is not along the shortest path between two points, or "as the crow flies," but along a less direct route. We want to make this idea more precise by introducing a measure of distance in the plane that is called the *right-angle metric*. This defines the distance between the origin and a point having coordinates (x, y) to be $|x| + |y|$. Travel in this metric is along a horizontal distance $|x|$ followed by a vertical distance $|y|$, which is different from the conventional *Euclidean metric* distance defined by $\sqrt{x^2 + y^2}$. In an actual street pattern, the distance traveled would be somewhere between these extremes, but at the risk of being too conservative, we adopt the right-angle metric. Later computations will reveal that there is not a significant difference between the two (Exercise 3.5.3).

The locus of points in the x, y plane that are within a distance r of the origin is of course a circle of radius r, when using the Euclidean metric, and the area is πr^2; but, as a little thought will show, the corresponding locus of points that are within a distance r using the right-angle metric is now a square tilted by 90 degrees with sides of length $\sqrt{2}r$ and area $2r^2$ (Fig. 3.1).

If the travel speed of a fire truck is roughly constant, then response time is proportional to travel distance, and so from now on we work with distance traveled rather than elapsed time.

At this juncture we are able to compute the probability distribution of the travel distance D_1 between an incident and the closest responding fire company. (See Fig. 3.2 for an illustration of a typical situation.) Choose the coordinate system so that the incident is located at the origin. Since firehouses are Poissonly distributed in the region, the probability of there being no fire company within a distance r of the incident is simply $e^{-2\gamma r^2}$, using the fact that area in the right-angle metric is $2r^2$. Therefore, the probability that the closest unit is within a distance r is given by

$$F(r) = \text{prob}\,(D_1 \leq r) = 1 - \text{prob}\,(D_1 > r) = 1 - e^{-2\gamma r^2}. \qquad (3.6)$$

The density function of the random variable D_1 is obtained from Eq.(3.6) by differentiating $F(r)$ and is given by $F'(r) = 4\gamma r e^{-2\gamma r^2}$.

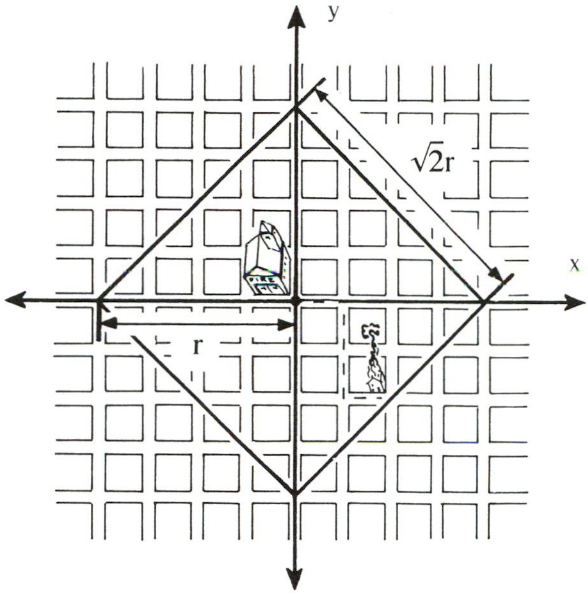

Figure 3.1. The right-angle distance metric.

The expected value of D_1 is now computed by the integral

$$E(D_1) = \int_0^\infty rF'(r)dr = 4\gamma \int_0^\infty r^2 e^{-2\gamma r^2} dr, \tag{3.7}$$

which is evaluated by rewriting Eq.(3.7):

$$E(D_1) = -2\gamma \frac{d}{d\gamma}\left(\int_0^\infty e^{-2\gamma r^2} dr\right).$$

Now make the substitution $x = \sqrt{2\gamma}\, r$ to obtain

$$\int_0^\infty e^{-2\gamma r^2} dr = \frac{1}{\sqrt{2\gamma}} \int_0^\infty e^{-x^2} dx,$$

and from a table of integrals we find that the last integral has the value $\sqrt{\pi}/2$. Putting all this together gives

$$E(D_1) = -\gamma(\pi/2)^{1/2} \frac{d}{d\gamma}\left(\frac{1}{\gamma^{1/2}}\right) = .627\gamma^{-1/2}. \tag{3.8}$$

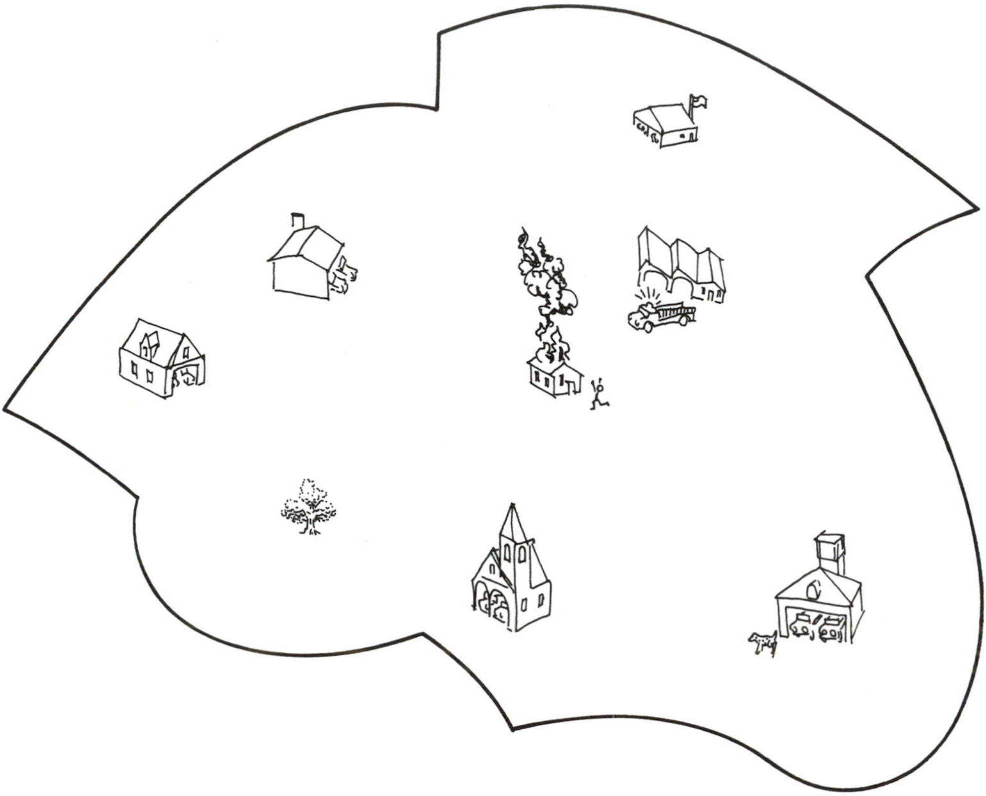

Figure 3.2. A hypothetical region with Poissonly distributed fire companies and an incident.

We therefore see that the expected travel distance is inversely proportional to the square root of the density γ of available units. This relation persists under a variety of assumptions about the distribution of response vehicles in the region and the metric one employs. It even continues to be valid if the kth closest fire company is dispatched instead of the nearest one. We can see this easily enough in the case of D_2, the distance to the second closest unit. The probability that the second closest is within a distance r of an incident, using the right-angle metric as before, is one minus the probability that either none or exactly one unit is within r. From the Poisson assumption about the distribution of firehouses, we obtain

$$G(r) = \text{prob}\,(D_2 \leq r) = 1 - e^{-2\gamma r^2} - 2\gamma r^2 e^{-2\gamma r^2},$$

with a density function given by $G'(r) = 8\gamma^2 r^3 e^{-2\gamma r^2}$. A computation like before (Exercise 3.5.4) yields

$$E(D_2) = \int_0^\infty rG'(r)dr = .941\gamma^{-1/2}. \tag{3.9}$$

Therefore, except for a slightly larger constant of proportionality, the expected value is the same as Eq.(3.8).

Since $\gamma = N/A(S)$, we can rewrite the expressions (3.8) and (3.9) as $c_1 N^{-1/2}$ and $c_2 N^{-1/2}$ for suitable constants, to make the dependence on N more explicit. These mean values assume that all N units are available to respond, which is unrealistic, since some fire companies could be busy on other calls. Let m be the number of busy units. In Section 3.2, we showed that the mean of the random variable m is λ/μ, and so the expected value of the variable $q = N - m$ is $E(q) = N - \lambda/\mu$. Conditioning on q, the number of units actually available, the expectation of D_1 is given by

$$E(D_1 \,|\, q) = c_1/q^{1/2}.$$

It is a standard result in probability theory (see Appendix A) that the unconditional mean of D_1 is the average of $E(D_1 \,|\, q)$ with respect to q, namely,

$$E(D_1) = E(E(D_1 \,|\, q)).$$

Now $1/q^{1/2}$ is, for $q > 0$, a convex function, meaning that the tangent line to the curve defined by the graph of the function lies on or below the curve itself (Fig. 3.3). Using simple calculus, one shows that, because of the convexity,

$$E(D_1) = E(E(D_1 \,|\, q)) \geq \frac{c_1}{E(q)^{1/2}} \tag{3.10}$$

(Exercise 3.5.6). If one is willing to hazard a possibly low estimate for the mean of D_1, the inequality in Eq.(3.10) can be replaced by an equality to give an expression for $E(D_1)$ in terms of the average number of available units:

$$E(D_1) = \frac{c_1}{(N - \lambda/\mu)^{1/2}}. \tag{3.11}$$

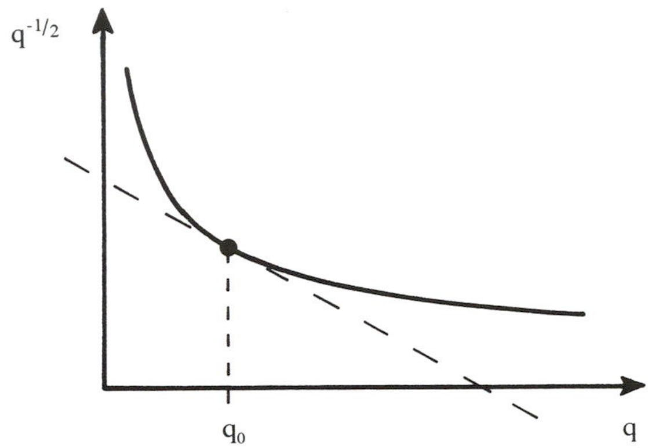

Figure 3.3. The convex function $1/q^{1/2}$ with a tangent line at some point q_0.

The same relation holds for D_2 except that the constant is replaced by c_2.

Empirical verification of Eq.(3.11) has been obtained by plotting actual response time data against the number of available units (see the paper by Kolesar and Blum in the references of Section 3.6), and it is remarkable that the relation persists in spite of the several tenuous assumptions that were made in its derivation, some acceptable, others perhaps less so, such as constant vehicle speed, uniform alarms in space, exponential service times, and a rectangular street grid. The robustness of Eq.(3.11) under a variety of conditions compels us to call it the *inverse square root law*, and it provides a simple link between available firefighting resources and the ability to respond to an alarm.

Let us close this section by considering what happens if the N companies in the region are assigned to only R firehouses, $R < N$, and that R_1 of the houses shelter one fire company and the remaining $R_2 = N - R_1$ harbor two. It follows, in this case, that $R_1 = 2R - N$ and $R_2 = N - R$. We make the simplifying assumption that all N companies are available to respond when an alarm arrives.

Observe that the average response distance of the closest unit is now $c_1 R^{-1/2}$, which is less than if all units had been dispersed among N houses instead of just R of them. For the second closest unit, however, the situation may be different. Roughly a fraction R_2/R of all alarms will have the second arriving fire company contained in the same house as the first arriving company, if the dispatch policy is to send two units to every alarm. This assumes, of course, that the two-company firehouses are scattered uniformly and not clustered in pockets within the region. R_2/R is an empirical estimate of the probability that both the first and second units to be dispatched come from the same house, and consequently have the same travel distance, while R_1/R is the corresponding probability that an alarm is answered by units residing in different houses. Therefore, by conditioning on these separate events, one obtains the average response distance of the second closest unit as

$$E(D_2) = R^{-1/2}\left(\frac{c_1 R_2}{R} + \frac{c_2 R_1}{R}\right).$$

Now suppose that $R_1 = 0$ so that all houses have two resident companies. Then $R = N/2$ and $E(D_2) = \sqrt{2}c_1/N^{1/2}$. But $c_1 = .627$ times the square root of the area while c_2 is .941 times the same factor, and so the travel distance of the second arriving unit is less than it would be if all units had been dispersed, one to a house. When $R_2 = 0$, on the other hand, $E(D_2)$ is larger than if the units had been scattered, as is easily verified. Overall response performance generally deteriorates, therefore, when R is less than N.

3.4. Optimal Deployment of Fire Companies

A city has been partitioned into k districts, and within each of these, fire alarms occur at random in a spatially uniform manner. These homogeneous sectors represent the different alarm histories that one can expect in diverse parts of the overall region, such as high- and low-density residential and business zones, where hazard rates vary with locale. Some sectors may also be determined by geography as, for example, when a river forms a natural barrier that separates one zone from another.

Calls in district i are assumed to come from a Poisson distribution at rate $\lambda_i, i = 1, 2, \ldots k$. The probability that the next citywide alarm actually originates from district i is, from Lemma 3.2, λ_i/λ , where λ is the sum of λ_1 through λ_k. For each i, let N_i be the number of fire companies assigned to the ith district and μ_i the average service time of companies in that district, which depends on travel conditions and the severity of fires. Service times are exponentially distributed.

Conditioning on the k disjoint events that an alarm arrives from sector i, the regionwide unconditional response distance D to the closest responding unit (our surrogate for response time) has an expected value that can be computed from formula (3.11):

$$E(D) = \sum_{i=1}^{k} \frac{c_i \lambda_i}{\lambda (N_i - \lambda_i/\mu_i)^{1/2}} = \sum_{i=1}^{k} g_i(N_i), \qquad (3.12)$$

where c_i equals .627 times the square root of the area of sector i. The Fire Department would like $E(D)$ to be as small as possible, and this leads to the optimization problem of minimizing this sum subject to the conditions that the N_i add up to N, the total available resources in the city, and that N_i be integers, at least one greater than the smallest integer in λ_i/μ_i. Once again, as in Chapter 2, this is an integer program, and it admits a simple solution. One begins by assigning the smallest possible number of units, $1 + [\lambda_i/\mu_i]$, to the ith term in Eq.(3.12). If this bare-bones deployment adds up to N, we are done. Otherwise, allocate one more unit to that term for which $g(N_i) - g(N_i + 1)$ is largest because this choice most decreases the sum. Continue in this fashion until all N available units have been assigned.

The resulting allocation is designed to optimize the citywide efficiency of deployment, but it may suffer in other respects. For example, a high-demand area with many fire alarms would receive somewhat more companies than would an adjacent sector that has fewer alarms, such as a low-density residential part of town. However, when a fire does occur in the residential area, the response time is likely to be greater, since the responding units are more dispersed. The taxpaying residents are understandably resentful of this inequity in coverage because they are being penalized for having fewer fires. Suppose then, in response to their outcry, that some additional units are permanently shifted to the residential zone. This leaves the high-density area more vulnerable than before, since travel times would tend to increase and, what is perhaps of equal significance, the workload of the fire companies in the high-demand area would exceed that of the companies in the adjoining region in the sense that each is busier a greater fraction of the time. The firefighters union would protest.

There is an evident need to reconcile the multiple and often conflicting interests of the city administration, the employees union, and community groups. While the citywide allocation based on the inverse square root law may fail to adequately meet the criteria of fairness imposed by citizens and firefighters (equity of coverage and equity of workload), it provides a compromise by placing more units in the high-demand areas while ensuring an acceptable level of coverage, and it has been used effectively by several municipalities as a rule of thumb for resource allocation. In New York City, for instance, during one of its recurrent fiscal crises, the Fire Department budget was cut and some fire companies had to be disbanded. Other units were then relocated to fill the resulting gaps in coverage by employing the inverse square root law to minimize the degradation in service caused by the cuts.

These changes were initially resisted by the firefighters as well as by community groups that felt threatened by the moves, but ultimately the cost-saving measures were implemented.(For further comments on this, see Section 3.6.)

One way to achieve equity of coverage is to temporarily reposition fire companies to other houses during periods of heavy demand. This relieves busy units and tends to reduce workload imbalances as well. The repositioning problem can be formulated mathematically by first partitioning a region into subzones called *response neighborhoods*, each of which is served by the two closest fire companies. Some firehouses may, of course, belong to more than one response neighborhood, assuming one company per firehouse, and so the partition consists of overlapping subzones.

A response neighborhood is uncovered if both of its closest units are busy on other calls, in which case some other available unit is temporarily assigned to one of the empty firehouses (Fig. 3.4). The problem now is to decide which of the empty houses to fill so as to minimize the number of relocated companies (Exercise 3.5.8). The issue here is not which of the available units to reposition, but rather,

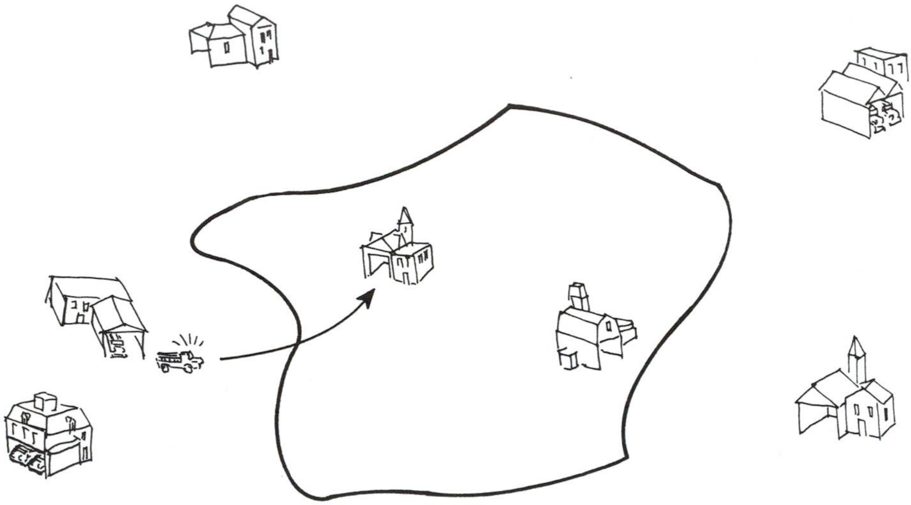

Figure 3.4. Illustration of repositioning with one unprotected response neighborhood and several adjacent firehouses. The arrow shows a deployable company being moved, temporarily, to the empty firehouse of a busy company.

how many, and is reminiscent of the integer programming problems considered in the previous chapter.

Part of the appeal of the inverse square root law is that while deceptively simple to state and to use, it is a surprisingly effective tool for planning the long-term deployment of firefighting resources. However, there are other short-term deployment issues concerning day-to-day operations that are also of considerable interest, and we touch on them briefly next.

Although we have assumed that one always dispatches the nearest unit to an alarm, it is not obvious that sending a more distant unit could sometimes be more effective in the long run. Usually, the optimal response is to deploy the closest unit (or units); but during a busy period in a high-demand area, this dispatch policy could strip the immediate area of all its firefighting resources, and a future alarm might well be answered by a unit that is considerably more distant. Therefore, if the closest unit is not dispatched initially to an alarm, the delay in response time experienced by the incident could

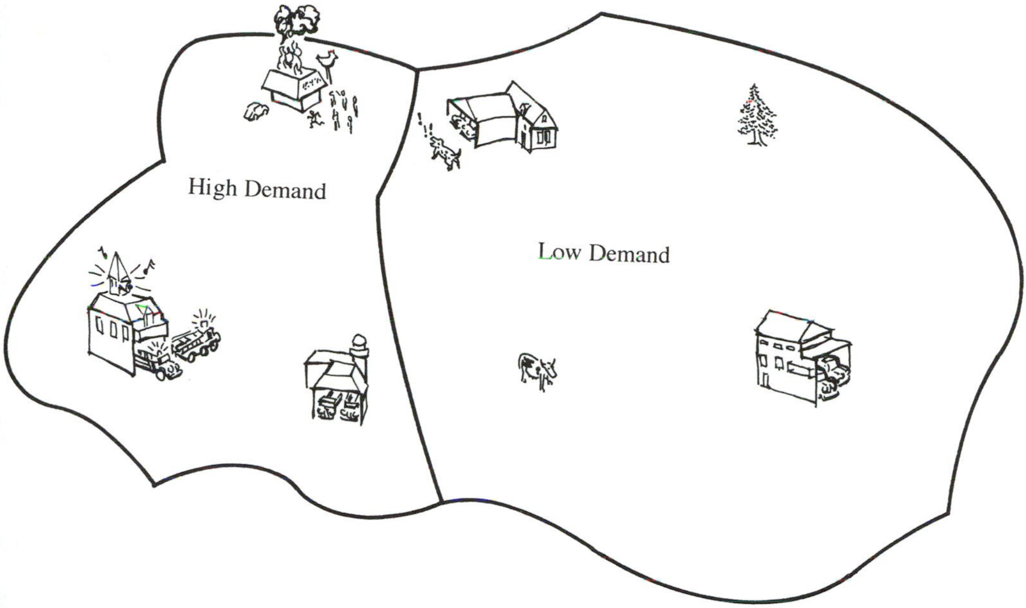

Figure 3.5. Adjacent high- and low-demand areas with boundaries drawn so that the first responding unit is not necessarily the closest unit.

be compensated for by the ability of that unit to be available for future alarms. There is a trade-off here between the short-term advantage in responding quickly to a current alarm and the long-term gain in having units available to send to future incidents. The problem is to decide on how to place the boundary of the response sector of a first responding unit so that an exceptionally busy company has a smaller response zone than would a company in a lower-alarm area. With appropriately redefined boundaries, any workload imbalance is reduced, and there would be an occasional exception to the rule of sending the closest unit. (See Fig. 3.5 for an illustration of this idea.) This is in contrast to the repositioning problem considered earlier, in which boundaries were drawn to specifically include the closest (and second closest) units.

Intimately connected with the question of which units to send is that of how many to send. Suppose that one or two units are dispatched to any alarm. (At large fires, even more units could be deployed, but for simplicity we ignore that possibility here.) It is sometimes difficult to gauge the severity of a fire, which could even be a false alarm, until the first company to arrive at the scene makes a determination. There is a trade-off here between sending two units initially and finding that only one is needed (a minor brush fire, for example), or initially sending one to a fire that may in fact be serious. In the first instance, one of the units is temporarily unavailable to respond elsewhere, while in the other situation there is a delay before a much-needed second unit finally arrives. The delay in the availability of firefighting units increases the risk of loss to life and property, and so the problem is to decide, based on the likelihood that a fire is serious (as determined from the past "alarm history" of the region) and on the number of units already busy at other incidents, how many to send to a new alarm.

These tactical questions of how many and which units to dispatch can be formulated mathematically, but we do not do so here. (See, however, the references in Section 3.6).

3.5. Exercises

3.5.1. The expected value of a Poisson random variable $N(t)$ at rate λ is λt, and if T is exponentially distributed at rate μ, then the expected value of T is $1/\mu$. Show this.

3.5.2. Let T_i be the successive gaps in the arrivals of a Poisson process at rate λ. Using Eq.(3.3), show that

$$\text{prob}\left(\sum_{i=1}^{k} T_i > t\right) = \sum_{j=0}^{k-1} (\lambda t)^j \frac{e^{-\lambda t}}{j!}$$

with an expected value of k/λ.

3.5.3. Formula (3.8) was derived assuming a right-angle distance metric. Using very similar arguments, rederive the expected value of D_1 in terms of the Euclidean metric, in which the distance between two points in the plane is the square root of the sum of the squares of the distances along each coordinate direction. Show that $E(D_1) = .5\gamma^{-1/2}$.

3.5.4. Complete the derivation of formula (3.9) for $E(D_2)$. Extend this result to obtain the expected distance to the kth nearest vehicle.

3.5.5. Compute the variance of D_1 in the right-angle metric. *Hint:* Var $(D_1) = E(D_1^2) - E(D_1)^2$ and prob $(D_1^2 \leq r)$ = prob $(D_1 \leq \sqrt{r})$.

3.5.6. In Section 3.4, we saw that $1/q^{1/2}$ is a convex function (Fig. 3.3). Denote this function by $h(q)$. To establish the inequality (3.10) in the text, recall that the convexity of h means that the tangent to the curve $(q, h(q))$ in the plane always lies on or below the curve itself. If $q_0 > 0$ is some given point, the equation of the tangent line at q_0 is $t(q) = h(q_0) + h'(q_0)(q - q_0)$, where $h'(q_0)$ denotes the derivative of h, namely, the slope of the tangent line, at q_0. Therefore, convexity means that

$$h(q) \geq h(q_0) + h'(q_0)(q - q_0) \text{ for all } q_0 > 0.$$

Now let $q_0 = E(q)$ and establish Eq.(3.10), which can be restated more compactly as $E(h(q)) \geq h(E(q))$. *Hint: Recall the properties of a mean value of a nonnegative random variable.*

3.5.7. Optimization of the citywide deployment of fire companies using formula (3.12) guarantees a level of efficiency that slights other considerations of equity, as discussed in Section 3.4. A modification of Eq.(3.12) offers a partial way out of the dilemma. Replace each of the expressions $(N_i - \lambda_i/\mu_i)^{-1/2}$, which we rewrite as $f(N_i)$ for short, by $f(N_i)^b$, where b is a nonnegative parameter. When $b = 1$, one recovers Eq.(3.12), but if b is taken to be smaller than one, then each term in the sum becomes less dependent on response distance, especially as b gets closer to zero. On the other hand, choosing b bigger than one, the opposite occurs and, as b gets larger and larger, the terms with the larger travel distances begin to dominate the sum. Explain how the conflicting measures of performance — namely, efficiency of coverage, workload imbalance, and coverage imbalance, all discussed in Section 3.4 — can be traded off against each other by letting b vary over nonnegative values. Having chosen a value of b, the suitably modified form of Eq.(3.12) is then minimized as before.

3.5.8. The repositioning problem discussed in Section 3.4 can be written as an integer program, similar to those discussed in the previous chapter. (See also Fig. 3.4.) Let $a_{i,j}$ equal one if the jth busy company belongs to the ith uncovered response neighborhood, and zero otherwise. Also, define x_j to be one if the empty firehouse of the jth busy company is to be temporarily filled by repositioning some other available unit. We wish to minimize the number of companies that must be relocated subject to the condition that no response neighborhoods remain uncovered. Express this mathematically.

3.5.9. A contagious disease (such as smallpox) has a lengthy incubation period so that a newly infected person manifests no symptoms for a period of time that we take to be exponentially distributed, with an average asymptomatic latency period of $1/\mu$. Each infected person that shows no symptoms can infect other susceptible individuals. The number of individuals infected this way is a counting process that is assumed to be Poisson at a rate λ that depends on the frequency of contact between susceptibles and infectives as well as the intimacy of contact. Even social customs may affect this rate, as, for example, whether people who meet embrace or simply nod to each other politely. There is a superficial resemblance here to the fire department problem in which the number of new infectives are arriving alarms and the incubation period is the service time of a busy fire company. Following the discussion in Section 3.2, show that the probability of exactly k new susceptibles becoming infected during the period in which no sick person shows any symptoms is $(\lambda/(\lambda+\mu))^k(\mu/(\lambda+\mu)$, with an average number of new infectives being λ/μ. *Hint: Recall the properties of the geometric distribution (Exercise 1.5.1).*

3.5.10. Continuing with the previous exercise, let $\Theta = \lambda/\mu$ and assume that $\Theta < 1$. Each generation of infectives behaves in the same way as the previous one, and if W_m denotes the number of infectives in the mth generation, then, since there are W_{m-1} infectives in the previous generation,

$$W_m = \sum_{i=1}^{W_{m-1}} U_i,$$

where U_i is the number of cases transmitted by the ith infective. The expected value of U_i, regardless of m, is Θ, as we saw in the previous exercise; that is, $E(U_i \mid W_{m-1}) = \Theta$. Using the same result about conditional means that was employed in deriving Eq.(3.10), namely that $E(W_m) = E(E(W_m \mid W_{m-1}))$, as discussed in Appendix A, it follows that

$$E(W_m) = E(\sum_{i=1}^{W_{m-1}} \Theta) = \Theta E(W_{m-1}).$$

Now $W_0 = 1$, since all infectives come from a single sick person in the zeroth generation. Therefore, we can solve for W_m recursively. Using this, compute the total average number of infectives produced by the first sick person. Throughout these computations, it has been assumed that once a sick person manifests symptoms, he or she is removed from society by quarantine or hospitalization and so no longer transmits the disease to anyone else.

Finally, establish that the epidemic eventually dies out by verifying that prob $(W_m = 0) \to 1$ as $m \to \infty$

3.5.11. In this chapter, we worked with response distance D rather than response time T. Both are random variables, and so is the speed of travel S of a fire engine. Since it is true that $T = D/S$, it was assumed that $E(T) = E(D)/E(S)$; but in fact, $E(T) = E(D)E(1/S)$ and $1/S$ is a convex function of S. Using arguments similar to those in Exercise 3.5.6, show that actually $E(T) \geq E(D)/E(S)$.

3.5.12. We are given a region of area A as shown in Fig. 3.6, in which a firehouse is located at the center, where the x and y coordinates are zero. An incident occurs at random uniformly within the region, and a vehicle

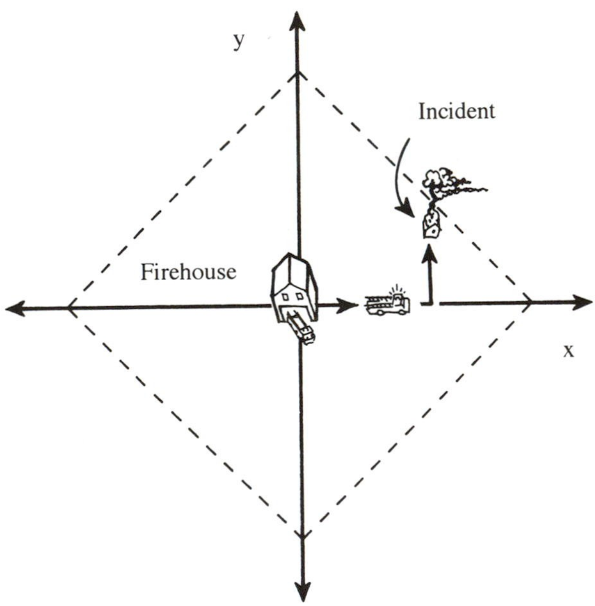

Figure 3.6.

is dispatched from the firehouse along a right-angle distance metric. A typical path is indicated by dotted lines in Fig. 3.6. Compute the mean travel distance $E(D)$ to the incident. *Hint: The locus of points a distance r from the origin has area $2r^2$, and the probability that an incident is within distance r is therefore $2r^2/A$.*

3.6. Further Readings

There are a number of books on stochastic processes that discuss the Poisson distribution in detail, at a level commensurate with that adopted in this chapter. We can recommend the most recent edition of reference [13].

The inverse square root law for fire department operations was derived and tested in the paper by Kolesar and Blum [14], but a more comprehensive discussion of the models employed in this chapter, together with a thorough treatment of the Rand Fire Study, is in reference [15]. The question of which units to deploy to a given alarm is given a simple treatment for the case of two firehouses in the paper by Carter *et al.* [16], while the issue of how many to dispatch is fully discussed in [15]. The repositioning study is taken from [17].

As noted previously, the inverse square root law was a key tool in deciding how many fire companies to disband and how many to relocate during the fiscal crisis of New York City in 1971. This controversial move engendered protests at City Hall and a suit in Federal Court by the firefighters union and by irate citizens. However, after the analysis was explained in court and at briefings to local groups, the opposition died down and the changes took place at a considerable savings to the city. (See "Union fights Fire Department Cuts," *New York Times*, Dec. 22, 1972.)

The Poisson distribution has wide applicability in the modeling of stochastic processes. This is illustrated in Exercises 3.5.9 and 3.5.10, which discuss a model for the spread of an infectious disease. Further details on this topic are available in the little booklet [18] and in the book by Bailey [20].

There is an amusing and perhaps unexpected connection with the question of fair allocation of scarce resources in a municipality or, in the context of Chapter 2, in the assignment of congressional seats, to problems posed in the Talmud concerning the fair division of an estate among heirs.

In the simplest setting two entities vie for a share of some scarce resource. This could be two urban districts needing an assignment of fire companies, or states that require congressional seats. The total number of fire units or seats, as the case may be, is limited. More abstractly, suppose that the two entities claim amounts s_1 and s_2 from a total s, with $s_i \leq s, i = 1, 2$, and $s_1 + s_2 \geq s$. If claimant i get what it asks for, it concedes an amount $s - s_i$ to the other. What remains at issue, therefore, is an amount $s - (s - s_1) - (s - s_2) = s_1 + s_2 - s$. In a captivating paper by Aumann and Maschler [21] it is shown, using game-theoretic notions, that the way to proceed is for the two protagonists to split the difference $s_1 + s_2 - s$ between them evenly and, in addition, to relinquish to i the conceded amount $s - s_j, j = 3 - i$.

An ancient dispute and its resolution is reported in the Talmud as "two hold a garment; one claims it all, the other claims half. Then the one is awarded three quarters, the other one quarter." This is precisely the rule formulated above, and, when suitably extended, it shows that a fair division among multiple claimants will continue to be fair when restricted to any subset of claimants. In particular, it provides the contested garment solution for any two contenders.

When applied to the congressional apportionment problem, for example, it meets some of the criteria for fair representation in the sense that any apportionment that is acceptable to all states remains acceptable to any subset of states being considered. Hamilton's approtionment scheme, discussed in Section 2.3, violated this criterion, although it was met by the proposals of Jefferson and Webster. An example of this lack of uniformity is illustrated by the case of Oklahoma, which became a state in 1907. Up to that time, the house consisted of 386 seats, apportioned, according to Hamilton's method, so that New York had 38 members and Maine 3. Oklahoma's entry entitled it to 5 seats, which it received, and the new house size was 391. However, under Hamilton's method, New York would now be forced to give up one seat in favor of Maine for a total of 37 in New

York and 4 in Maine, even though the population of each state had not changed.

Caution must be exercised in applying these ideas to the municipal deployment problems that were considered in this and the preceding chapter, since the concept of fair division can have different meanings for urban services.

4

Measles and Sardines

4.1. Background

In his novel *Cannery Row*, John Steinbeck vividly describes the bustle of a sardine factory in Monterey, California, before the Second World War, when heavily laden boats brought in the abundant catch of the sea; but the industry suffered a sharp decline as the sardine population collapsed in the late 1940s and the once thriving canneries began to close down. Later, in the early 1970s, a similarly precipitous drop in the catch of anchovies occurred in Peru, then the largest fishery in the world. What happened? Although some episodic shift in climate may have had an influence, especially the influx of warm waters known as *el niño*, which occurs sporadically off the Peruvian coast, the dominant factor in each instance was, quite simply, overfishing.

When commercial fishing begins along some coastal region, this sets in motion an investment in fishing gear that continues to increase to exploit what initially appears to be an ample natural resource, and within a few years a sizable fleet plies the waters. As fish stocks dwindle and prices rise, the competition among fishermen intensifies, and even more aggressive fishing tactics may be the response. Certain species of fish, such as sardines, anchovies, and herring, swim in schools that not only favor their detection and bulk harvest, but, in biological terms, their ability to breed may be diminished by low population densities. This implies that an overly exploited species can have a diminished capacity to recruit new adults. In Section 4.4, a model is presented that combines both economic and biological considerations and that exhibits how the sudden collapse of just such a species becomes possible as a critical level of harvesting is reached.

The setting now shifts to a crowded schoolroom in winter, where one child after another comes down with a rash and fever, a case of measles. From time to time, epidemics of childhood diseases such as measles arise in cities around the country, most recently during the late 1980s. This, too, is a form of harvesting, in which susceptible individuals fall victim to a contagious disease when they encounter others who are already infected. The analogy with fishing is admittedly a bit farfetched, but there is in fact a whole class of problems, in which two or more species interact through exploitation or competition or conflict, that can be formulated mathematically in quite similar ways. Grim warfare, territorial disputes among birds, the hide-and-seek behavior of predators and their victims, and even chemical reactions are all manifestations of species that intermingle because they are in the same place at the same time.

What the mathematical models of these processes have in common is that they record changes that take place over time and, as we will see in a later chapter, in space as well, and are described in terms of rates of change, such as the rate of reproduction, rate of becoming infected, rate of harvesting; but rates imply derivatives, and so it is not surprising that the models are expressed as differential equations, a vast and sometimes difficult subject from which we extract a few essential ideas in the next section, enough so that we can gain some insight into an assortment of models. In addition to using analytical tools to reveal the behavior of solutions to the differential equations, it is also expedient to employ computer-generated graphics to display the numerically integrated solutions. This will be done throughout this chapter and the next. The epidemic model itself is discussed in

Section 4.5, where we obtain a brief glimpse of chaotic dynamics, a topic of considerable current interest.

An interesting form of competition is in the marketplace, where the struggle is among business competitors. In Section 4.3, a simplified model of a marketplace is presented in which goods are bought and sold. Each producer tries to obtain the highest possible price for an item sold, while each consumer of goods attempts to pay the least. Supply and demand are both functions of price, and the question is whether the use of bargaining will ever drive the prices to a level at which supply and demand are in balance.

We encountered competition in the form of political leverage in earlier chapters. This implies that there is another, more subtle, side to the raw claw-for-claw struggle for dominance that pervades many of the models that we elaborate on here, namely, the use of negotiation and even cooperation to achieve goals that elude an all-or-nothing approach to survival. We return to this idea in Chapter 6.

4.2. Equilibria and Stability

Since all the models in this chapter involve differential equations, we need to discuss some of the properties of simultaneous first order ordinary differential equations in k dependent variables $x_i(t)$, $1 \leq i \leq k$. The x_i define the states of a dynamical system in terms of an independent variable t that is regarded as time:

$$\begin{aligned} x_1' &= f_1(x_1, ... x_k), \\ &\vdots \\ x_k' &= f_k(x_1, ... x_k). \end{aligned} \tag{4.1}$$

The superscript prime denotes differentiation with respect to t (we suppress, for notational convenience, the explicit dependence on t in Eq.(4.1) and in what follows), and the f_i are generally nonlinear functions of the k variables. A specific example of what we have in mind is the following system of two equations, a variant of which will be considered in the subsequent section:

$$\begin{aligned} x_1' &= rx_1(1-x_1) - x_1x_2, \\ x_2' &= x_2(px_1 - c), \end{aligned} \tag{4.2}$$

where r, p, and c are positive constants. The nonlinearity comes about from the fact that the right side of the equations include products of the variables. Other examples will follow later, but for the moment our discussion is necessarily more abstract.

A compact version of Eq.(4.1) is

$$x' = f(x), \tag{4.3}$$

which is obtained by using the vector notation

$$\mathbf{x}(t) = \begin{pmatrix} x_1(t) \\ \vdots \\ x_k(t) \end{pmatrix}, \quad \mathbf{x}'(t) = \begin{pmatrix} x_1'(t) \\ \vdots \\ x_k'(t) \end{pmatrix}, \quad \text{and} \quad \mathbf{f}(x) = \begin{pmatrix} f_1(t) \\ \vdots \\ f_k(t) \end{pmatrix}.$$

The vector $\mathbf{x}(t)$ defines the state of the dynamical system at any time t, and it traces out a solution curve in k-dimensional space, called a *trajectory*, that describes how the system moves in time.

We assume that the equations are an adequate representation of an observable process, and so on purely intuitive grounds it is reasonable to expect that the equations have solutions that mimic the actual time evolution of the process itself. Specifically, we assume that if the state is prescribed to have a value x_0 at some initial time $t = 0$, then there is a unique vector valued function $\mathbf{x}(t)$ defined for all time t, which passes through x_0 at $t = 0$. Precise conditions on the vector function $\mathbf{f}$ can be given that guarantee that a unique solution with these properties does indeed exist, but we forgo the details, since we already believe that the equations are well-posed in terms of the processes that they describe. Section 4.2 of the book by Redheffer, mentioned in Section 4.7, fills in the mathematical details that are sidestepped here. The uniqueness requirement is especially significant, since it tells us that the time evolution of a dynamical system along individual trajectories follows distinct paths; if two trajectories were to cross each other, then their point of contact is an initial state from which two separate solutions emerge, a violation of uniqueness.

Equations (4.1) and (4.3) are first-order systems, since each involves only the variables x_i and their first derivatives. A single kth order equation that has derivatives up to order k can always be reduced to a set of k first-order equations. For example, the second-order equation

$$y'' + \sin y = 0$$

becomes

$$\begin{aligned} x_1' &= x_2, \\ x_2' &= -\sin x_1 \end{aligned}$$

when we let $x_1 = y$ and $x_2 = y'$.

Some solutions remain constant in time. These states of rest are called *equilibrium solutions* and are defined by positions x for which the time derivative x' is zero. At an equilibrium, no motion ensues. In Eqs.(4.2), for example, the equilibrium states are the vectors

$$\begin{pmatrix} 0 \\ 0 \end{pmatrix}, \quad \begin{pmatrix} c/p \\ 0 \end{pmatrix}, \quad \text{and} \quad \begin{pmatrix} c/p \\ r - rc/p \end{pmatrix}.$$

Our concern is with knowing what happens to a trajectory as time evolves. An equilibrium state q is called an *attractor*, and is said to be *asymptotically stable*, if all trajectories that begin in some sufficiently small neighborhood of q approach the equilibrium arbitrarily close as t increases. More specifically, there is a set Ω of initial states x_0 such that the solution through x_0 will lie in an arbitrarily small neighborhood of q when t is large enough. The largest set Ω for which this is true is called the *basin of attraction* of q. A state q may fail to be a point attractor if trajectories that begin close enough to q remain confined to some bounded neighborhood of q for all time but do not actually tend to q. In this case, we say that q is stable, but not asymptotically stable, whereas if no such bounded neighborhood exists, then q is called *unstable.* An unstable equilibrium repels at least one trajectory in its neighborhood.

There are attractors other than equilibria. Trajectories that begin in some set Ω of initial states may, for example, tend toward a closed orbit that represents a periodic solution of the differential equations.

An illustration of this is provided by the equations

$$\begin{aligned} x_1' &= x_2 - \left(\frac{x_1^3}{3} - x_1\right), \\ x_2' &= -x_1, \end{aligned}$$

whose solutions in x_1, x_2 space are plotted in Fig. 4.1. There is a single equilibrium state at the origin that is unstable, since it repels all trajectories in its neighborhood. These trajectories spiral outward to the cyclic trajectory, while all solutions that begin outside the closed orbit eventually wind down towards it.

There are other, more complicated examples of attractors, but our

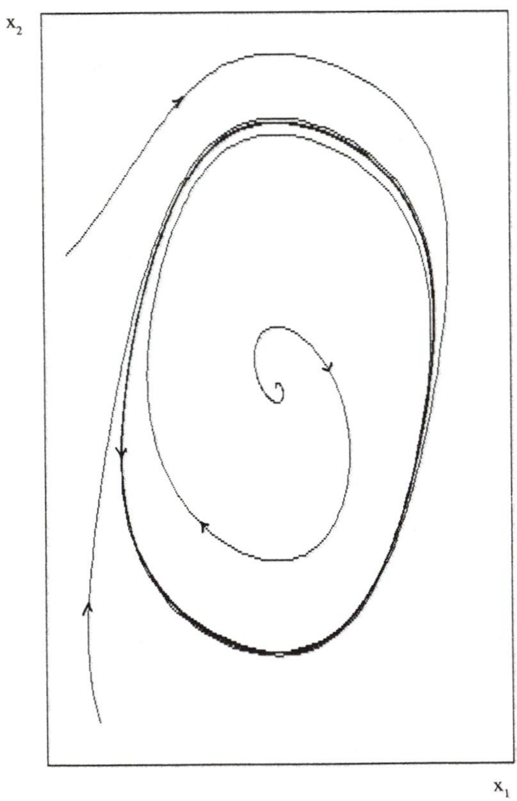

Figure 4.1. A closed orbit is a periodic attractor.

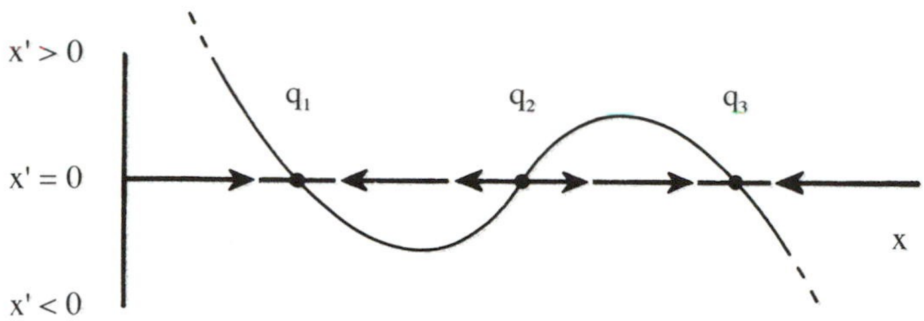

Figure 4.2. Stable and unstable equilibria.

attention will be largely confined to asymptotically stable equilibria.

Our task now is to identify point attractors of specific equation systems. The simplest case is that of a single nonlinear equation in which x is a scalar function ($k = 1$). Although it is sometimes possible to solve the equations explicitly, there are many interesting cases in which there is a simpler, more direct approach to the question of what happens to trajectories as t increases. One begins by finding the equilibria of $x' = f(x)$ which is the algebraic problem of finding the roots of the equation $f(x) = 0$. If q is one such root, consider the sign of $f(x)$ in a neighborhood of q. If $f(x)$, and therefore the derivative of $x(t)$, is positive, this tells us that x is increasing, whereas a negative sign indicates that $x(t)$ is decreasing. In Fig. 4.2, we consider a typical $f(x)$ that crosses the x axis at three points q_1, q_2, and q_3. These are the equilibria of $x' = f(x)$, and by looking at the sign of f, we immediately verify that q_1 and q_3 are attractors and q_2 is unstable. The arrows indicate the direction of the one-dimensional trajectory $x(t)$.

To make our discussion more concrete, we now derive an equation that models a growth and decay process of considerable interest. An organism is assumed to grow at a constant per capita rate r. This means that the net difference in the rate of births and deaths, per unit of population, is constant. Thus, if three cells per thousand divide every minute and one per thousand dies, the per capita rate r is .002. Let $x(t)$ denote the total population at time t, with an initial count of $x(0) = x_0$. Taking r to be positive, the rate of increase in population is simply $x'(t) = rx(t)$. This differential equation has a correspondingly simple solution, as is readily verified: $x(t) = x_0 \exp(rt)$. It predicts that the population grows exponentially from its initial value. Although this is roughly true for a number of species for relatively short periods of their history, including humans, it grossly exaggerates what happens over longer time spans. A better model is obtained by recognizing that as a population grows, the eventual overcrowding causes the birth rate to decline and the death rate to increase because of disease and aggressive competition for dwindling resources. This suggests that a constant r should be replaced by a per capita rate that decreases as population increases. A plausible candidate is obtained by replacing r with $rx(1 - x/K)$, where K represents the theoretically maximum population that can be sustained in a given habitat. Suppose now that the population is subject to exploitation, such as a fishery, or to predation, such as algae in the ocean that are grazed on by small crustaceans, or even emigration from a region in the case of humans. Let $E > 0$ denote the per capita rate of removal of the species from the region in which it finds itself. Then the equation for the rate of growth of the population becomes

$$x' = rx\left(1 - \frac{x}{K}\right) - Ex. \tag{4.4}$$

The first term on the right is the net growth of the species due to its own internal dynamics of birth and death, while the second term captures the external effect of movement across the region's boundary. Incidently, if E is taken to be negative, this represents a net inflow into the region, such as immigration for humans or the restocking of a fishery, or a massive migration of algae into a part of the ocean due to a sudden shift in the current.

Equation (4.4) can be rewritten as

$$x' = (r - E)x(1 - x/K(1 - E/r)),$$

and there are evidently two equilibria, at $x = 0$ and $x = K(1 - E/r)$. If one graphs the right side of the equation, namely, $f(x)$, it is seen that it is positive between zero and $K(1 - E/r)$ and negative otherwise. From this, we deduce, as before, that zero is unstable while $K(1 - E/r)$ is an attractor. This means that the population will inevitably increase from small values to a maximum value that approaches K as E is reduced to zero. Is this reasonable? In some situations, such as bacteria confined to a beaker supplied with nutrients, this seems to be what happens, and it is an acceptable approximation for human populations as well. However, the model is based on several questionable assumptions that suggest caution in its use. We return to this in the next section, but for now our goal is to examine the mathematical side of this and other nonlinear equations.

An alternative approach to deciding whether an equilibrium is attracting is based on the idea of approximating the nonlinear equation $x' = f(x)$ by a linear equation that is readily solved. If q is an equilibrium state, Taylor's theorem in the calculus allows us to write $f(x)$ as $f(q) + f'(q)(x-q)+$ higher-order terms in $x - q$. (We assume that f is a twice differentiable function.) For x sufficiently close to q, the higher-order terms are negligible, and so if one ignores the terms in $(x-p)^2$ and higher, the original equation can be approximated by the linear equation $u' = au$, where $a = f'(q)$ and $u = x - q$. (Recall that $f(q) = 0$.) This provides a *linearization* of $x' = f(x)$ about the equilibrium q, and it is reasonable to conjecture that in a neighborhood of q, the solution of the nonlinear equation shadows the linearized solution. Equation $u' = au$ has the solution $u(t) = u_0 \exp(at)$, where u_0 is the initial value of u, namely, $x(0) - q$. If a is negative, it is apparent that $u(t)$ tends to zero, its equilibrium solution, as t goes to infinity. When a is positive, the solution grows without bound and the origin is unstable. Now a movement of u towards zero is tantamount to x going to q, and so it would seem that q is an attractor for the nonlinear equation if zero is an attractor for its linearized version. This leads to the next result, which verifies our conjecture:

Lemma 4.1. *Let q be an equilibrium of the scalar equation $x' = f(x)$, where f is twice differentiable and let $a = f'(q)$. Then q is an attractor if $a < 0$ and it is unstable if $a > 0$.*

Proof. Let $u = x - q$ to write the equation $x' = f(x)$ as

$$u' = au + g(u),$$

where $g(u)$ represents terms in u of order two and higher. The function g satisfies $g(0) = 0$ and $g'(0) = 0$. Moreover, g' is continuous and, therefore, for any given ϵ, $|g'(u)| < \epsilon$ for all $|u| < \delta$, where δ is suitably small; but

$$g(u) = \int_0^u g'(s)ds,$$

and so $|g(u)| < \epsilon|u|$ when $|u| < \delta$. Suppose that a is negative. Then $a < -\epsilon$ for ϵ small enough. This means that $u' = au + g(u) < -\epsilon u + \epsilon u = 0$, provided that $0 < u < \delta$. In the same way, u' is positive if $-\delta < u < 0$. In either case, it follows that if $|u| < \delta$ initially, then $u(t)$ goes to zero as t increases. When a is positive, a similar argument shows that the origin is unstable. The result follows by noting that $x = u + q$. □

Thus, we have resolved the issue of stability or instability for the case of scalar equations. Of course, one can sometimes, though not always, explicitly solve the equation and thereby obtain the long-term behavior of the solutions directly, as in the case of Eq.(4.4) (Exercise 4.6.1), but as soon as we go beyond the case of single equations to systems, the likelihood of an explicit solution is sharply reduced and one is constrained to use surrogate methods. We illustrate one such technique for pairs of equations ($k = 2$) that turns out to be a two-dimensional analogue of what we did before in the scalar case. To be specific, we consider the situation of coupled equations that model the competition of two species that cohabit a given region with populations of x_1 and x_2, respectively. Each species can thrive in isolation from the other and separately follow a growth law of the form (4.4) in which $E = 0$. In the biological literature, this is known as a *logistic equation.* However, when the two species are forced to compete with each other for food and other limited resources, each inhibits the other and diminishes the ability of either of them to fully prosper. This a form of mutual exploitation that we model by terms that are proportional to the product of their populations, since this measures the likelihood of an encounter between them:

$$\begin{aligned} x_1' &= rx_1\left(1 - \frac{x_1}{K}\right) - ax_1x_2, \\ x_2' &= sx_2\left(1 - \frac{x_2}{L}\right) - bx_1x_2. \end{aligned} \tag{4.5}$$

All constants are positive in which s is the intrinsic per capita growth rate of the second species and L is the maximum population level it can theoretically sustain within the given region. The coefficients a and b measure the competitive advantage of one species over another. As a increases, for example, this indicates that the second species becomes more effective in outwitting, subduing, or otherwise inhibiting its competitor. Of course, this model is only a caricature of what really takes place between two or more species, and its utility lies in the fact that it is a widely adopted paradigm of the raw struggle for dominance in nature. We will have occasion to treat a generalization of these equations in a later chapter that explicitly includes the effect of movement in space, something that is only implicit in the present version in which the spatial background is "frozen."

Equations (4.5) have several equilibria. The algebraic equations obtained by letting x_1' and x_2' be zero separately are called *nullclines*, and the intersections of these nullclines are the points in the plane where the equilibrium states occur, since both of the right-hand sides are simultaneously zero there. An easy computation shows that there are four possibilities for equilibria in the positive quadrant. (Any solution with either of the x_i negative makes no sense physically and is disregarded.) To begin with, there is the uninteresting case in which both species are zero, then two possibilities in which one or the other species, but not both, is zero, and the case in which the nullclines intersect at a positive value for both species. We pick a specific situation and consider parameters for which $r/L < a$ and $s/K < b$. This forces the nullclines to intersect in the positive quadrant, where neither species is zero. This is shown in Fig. 4.3. Other possibilities are considered in Exercise 4.6.3. We now return to the idea of looking at the sign of the derivatives, a ploy that worked so well for us in the case of a single scalar equation.

Factor out the positive equilibrium values of x_1 and x_2 from the right-hand sides of Eqs.(4.5). The nullclines are the straight lines exhibited in Fig. 4.3, and a little reflection shows that if x_1 has a value that lies to the right of the line defined by $x_2' = 0$, then the derivative of x_2 is negative, while if its value lies to the left of this line, the derivative is positive. Similarly, when x_2 is a value that lies above the line defined by nullcline $x_1' = 0$,then the derivative of x_1 is negative and it changes sign when x_2 is below the line.

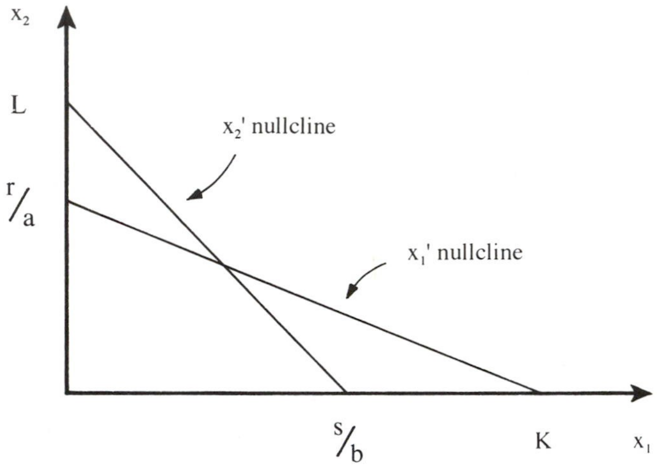

Figure 4.3. Nullclines for the competition model equations in (4.5).

The signs of the derivatives tell us, of course, whether the variables x_1 and x_2 are increasing or decreasing, and this gives us a clue to the direction of flow of the solution curves, namely, the trajectories. Note that these curves must cross the nullclines either vertically or horizontally. For example, if $x_1' = 0$, it means that there is no change in the x_1 variable and so the trajectory must be vertical as it crosses the nullcline defined by this zero derivative.

Putting all this information together permits one to make a crude sketch of the flow of the trajectories, a useful task that provides considerable insight into the dynamics of the model equations. To illustrate the method, consider the region that lies above and to the right of the two lines in Fig. 4.3. Both derivatives are negative here and so the flow is simultaneously downward and to the left. Since all trajectories are smooth curves (the functions f_i of the differential equations are assumed to be at least differentiable), the way in which they bend is determined by whether they must cross the nullclines horizontally or vertically. Some trajectories are forced to bend in one direction, while others bend in the opposite way. This is drawn in Fig. 4.4, where typical trajectories appear from all portions of the quadrant. Note that the horizontal and vertical axes represent valid

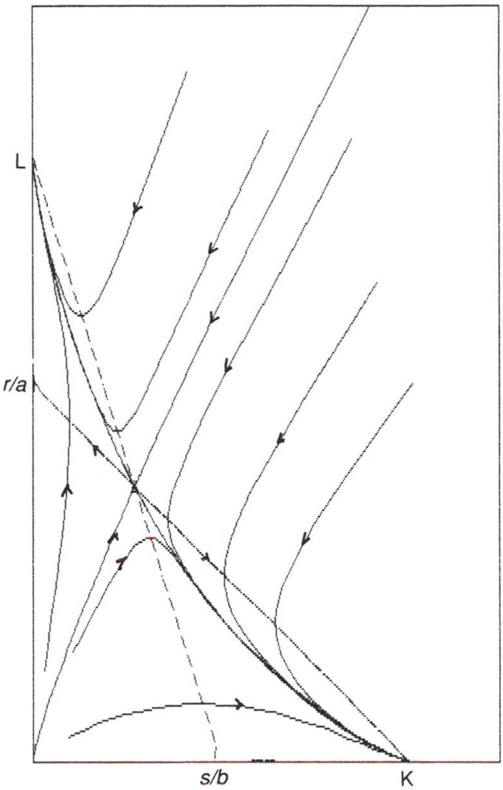

Figure 4.4. Trajectories for the competition model equations (4.5).

solutions to Eqs.(4.5), since these correspond to setting either x_1' or x_2' to zero. It follows that no trajectory that begins in the positive quadrant can ever leave this domain, for otherwise it would have to cross one of these axes and, as we observed earlier, this would violate the property of uniqueness of solutions. Therefore, the trajectories shown in Fig. 4.4 approach, but never actually reach, the equilibria.

Looking at Fig. 4.4, one sees that virtually all solutions tend to either of two attractors, in which one species or the other is zero, depending on their initial state. Apparently, the species intimidate each other sufficiently that one of them is eliminated, a phenomenon called *competitive exclusion*. The only exception to this occurs along the pair of curves that tend to the unstable equilibrium in which both species coexist. These curves define what is called a *separatrix*, since they separate all other trajectories into two mutually exclusive classes, those that tend to

$$\begin{pmatrix} 0 \\ L \end{pmatrix}$$

or to

$$\begin{pmatrix} K \\ 0 \end{pmatrix}.$$

This precariously delicate co-existence depends on choosing the initial values of the variables just right, an improbable feat. All states, other than those on the separatrix or the origin, belong to the basin of attraction of one of the two attractors. The origin is an unstable equilibrium.

In conclusion, we see that fierce competitiveness between two species inevitably leads to the extinction of one of them. In effect, they cannot occupy the same ecological niche. On the other hand, a different choice of the competition constants a, b in the model can lead to coexistence, implying that each species occupies distinct or, at most, partially overlapping niches. Competition, in this case, is mild (Exercise 4.6.3).

Another, more analytical approach to the same problem mimics the linearization procedure used earlier for scalar equations, but a discussion of this would require us to make a longer digression than is desirable. The intuitively satisfying nullcline approach outlined here will be a sufficiently good tool for the models that we deal with in this chapter.

4.3. Marketplace Dynamics

We now construct a simplified model of marketplace dynamics that serves as a metaphor for how an actual economy operates. The model is not only of interest in itself, but it allows us to introduce another approach to the problem of determining when equilibria are attractors.

We imagine the following situation that is a caricature of the way trading is done in a free market. People come to the marketplace with goods to trade. The willingness to buy or sell is dependent on the cost of each good, and so supply and demand are both functions of price. The question of interest here is whether the prices can ever be adjusted to a level at which supply and demand are in equilibrium. Let

$$\mathbf{p} = \begin{pmatrix} p_1 \\ \vdots \\ p_n \end{pmatrix}$$

be a set of prices for n different classes of commodities. The total demand and supply for commodity i at these prices are some generally nonlinear functions $d_i(p)$ and $s_i(p)$ that we need not specify. The excess demand for the ith commodity is then $f_i(p) = d_i(p) - s_i(p)$, and this gives rise to a vector $\mathbf{f}(p)$ whose n components are $f_i(p)$. If some arbitrary price vector $\mathbf{p}_0$ is announced at the beginning of the bargaining session, it is likely to be too high for some participants and too low for others. The premise we make is that the prices continuously adjust themselves over time through the bargaining process according to the rule

$$\mathbf{p}' = \mathbf{f}(\mathbf{p}),$$

where $\mathbf{p}$ is now thought of as a function of time t. Each component of $\mathbf{p}$ increases if the corresponding component of $\mathbf{f}(\mathbf{p})$ is positive, with the reverse if $\mathbf{f}(\mathbf{p})$ is negative.

This system of n differential equations is assumed to have a unique equilibrium at some price q. If we can show that q is an attractor, then it means that the prices would vary until the excess demand is zero, and in this case the market is deemed to be stable.

Trading takes place when the market reaches a stable equilibrium. The marketplace mimics a closed economy that is restricted to a fixed number of participants who are able to purchase some goods using only the cash obtained from the sale of some other goods. What this says, in effect, is that when prices are at an equilibrium the total cash used for purchases must equal the total cash obtained from sales.

If $\mathbf{p}' = \mathbf{f}(\mathbf{p})$ were a scalar equation, it would be easy to determine whether $\mathbf{q}$ is an attractor simply by looking at the sign of the derivative $\mathbf{p}'$, as we discussed earlier in the previous section. It is necessary to proceed differently in the vector case, however. To do this, consider the length of the squared Euclidean difference between $\mathbf{p}(t)$ and $\mathbf{q}$ at any time t:

$$D(\mathbf{p}(t)) = \frac{1}{2}||\mathbf{p}(t) - \mathbf{q}||^2 = \frac{1}{2}\sum_{i=1}^{n}(p_i(t) - q_i)^2,$$

where q_i is the ith component of the vector $\mathbf{q}$. The factor $\frac{1}{2}$ appears for mathematical convenience.

Differentiating $D(\mathbf{p}(t))$ with respect to t gives

$$D'(\mathbf{p}(t)) = \sum_{i=1}^{n}(p_i(t) - q_i)p_i'.$$

Since $p_i' = f_i$, we can rewrite this expression by using the notation $\mathbf{u}^T\mathbf{v}$ for the inner product of two column vectors $\mathbf{u}$ and $\mathbf{v}$:

$$D'(\mathbf{p}(t)) = (\mathbf{p}(t) - \mathbf{q})^T\mathbf{f}(\mathbf{p}) = \mathbf{p}(t)^T\mathbf{f}(\mathbf{p}) - \mathbf{q}^T\mathbf{f}(\mathbf{p}).$$

(see Appendix C on vector functions). The first term on the right is

$$\sum_{i=1}^{n} p_i(t)(d_i(p) - s_i(p)),$$

which represents the difference between aggregate income from the sale of goods and the aggregate expenditures due to consumption. Since our system is closed and total cash is conserved, the difference must be zero. This is known as *Walras' Law*, after the Swiss economist:

$$\mathbf{p}(t)^T\mathbf{f}(\mathbf{p}) = 0. \tag{4.6}$$

It now follows that $D'(\mathbf{p}(t)) = -\mathbf{q}^T\mathbf{f}(\mathbf{p})$, and we make the further assumption that this quantity is always negative for all $\mathbf{p}$ not equal to $\mathbf{q}$. This can be justified on plausible economic grounds (see, for example, the papers of Arrow and Hurwicz referred to in Section 4.7), but we do not do so here.

The negativity of D' implies that the distance between $\mathbf{p}(t)$ and $\mathbf{q}$ decreases over time and, as will be shown momentarily, $\mathbf{p}(t)$ actually tends to $\mathbf{q}$ from any initial value $\mathbf{p}_0$ in the state space of all possible prices. This makes $\mathbf{q}$ a global attractor.

Since $D(\mathbf{p}(t))$ is bounded below by zero (where $\mathbf{p} = \mathbf{q}$) and is strictly decreasing, it follows that it converges to some value $d \geq 0$.

We want to show that d is zero. Suppose, in fact that this value is actually positive. Since $\mathbf{D}(\mathbf{p}(t))$ is continuous in $\mathbf{p}(t)$ and non-zero, it follows that $||\mathbf{D}(\mathbf{p}(t))|| \geq s$ for some suitably small $s > 0$. Let $\mathbf{D}_r$ denote the set of all vectors $\mathbf{p}$ whose squared Euclidean distance from $\mathbf{q}$ is less than or equal to r, where r is strictly less than s: $\frac{1}{2}||\mathbf{p} - \mathbf{q}||^2 \leq r < s$. Then the trajectory $\mathbf{p}(t)$ never penetrates into the set $\mathbf{D}_r$. For any initial value $\mathbf{p}_0$,the distance to $\mathbf{q}$ is $R = \frac{1}{2}||\mathbf{p}_0 - \mathbf{q}||^2$, and it follows, for all times $t \geq 0$, that the trajectory lies in a closed and bounded set S defined by price vectors $\mathbf{p}$ that satisfy the inequalities $s \leq \frac{1}{2}||\mathbf{p} - \mathbf{q}||^2 \leq R$. The continous function $D'(\mathbf{p}(t))$ has a maximum on the set S that is strictly negative: $D'(\mathbf{p}(t)) < -\alpha$, for some positive α. Therefore,

$$D(\mathbf{p}(t)) = R + \int_0^t D'(\mathbf{p}(s))ds < R - \alpha t,$$

which goes to minus infinity as t increases. This contradicts the fact that $D(\mathbf{p}(t))$ is bounded below by s for all values of $\mathbf{p}(t)$, and so we conclude that d is indeed zero; the price trajectory tends to the attractor $\mathbf{q}$ and the market is stable.

The distance function D is an example of what is called a *Liapunov function* in honor of the Russian mathematician A.M. Liapunov, and the argument showing that D tends to zero is a version of *Liapunov's theorem*, a result that is used widely in the literature on differential equations. For a discussion of this topic, see Section 20.4 of the book by Redheffer mentioned in Section 4.7.

When the market has only two goods to trade, the analysis just given can be simplified considerably. First, note that we may assume $\mathbf{f}(0) > 0$ since net demand is always positive when the goods are free (zero price). Moreover, if c is any positive constant, then it is reasonable to expect that $\mathbf{f}(c\mathbf{p}) = \mathbf{f}(\mathbf{p})$. What this means is that if all prices are doubled, for example, then demand does not change. The reason is that although the value of the goods produced has doubled, it is also true that the goods to be purchased now also cost twice as much. Inflation catches up equally with both consumer and producer. Therefore, if two goods have prices p_1 and p_2 with a ratio $p_2/p_1 = r$, it follows that $f_2(p_1, p_2) = f_2(p_1, rp_1) = f_2(1, r)$, since we can factor out p_1 without changing the value of f_2, the second component of the vector $\mathbf{f}(\mathbf{p})$. It is convenient to write $f_2(p_1, p_2)$ as

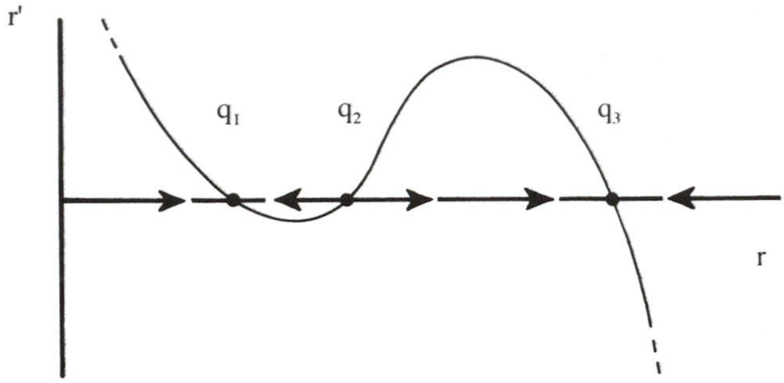

Figure 4.5. The derivative r' as a function of r, with three equilibria.

a function $g(r)$ of the ratio of prices. Similarly, from Eq.(4.6), we obtain $p_1 f_1 + p_2 f_2 = 0$, or $f_1(p_1, p_2) = -p_2 f_2(p_1, p_2)/p_1 = -rg(r)$. This gives us the differential equations for two goods:

$$\begin{aligned} p_1' &= -rg(r), \\ p_2' &= g(r). \end{aligned}$$

What we are after, however, is a differential equation for r. To do this, note that Eq.(4.6) can be expressed as

$$\mathbf{p}^T\mathbf{f}(\mathbf{p}) = \mathbf{p}^T\mathbf{p}' = \frac{1}{2}(\mathbf{p}^T\mathbf{p})' = 0,$$

since $\mathbf{p}' = \mathbf{f}(\mathbf{p})$. Therefore, $\mathbf{p}^T\mathbf{p} = p_1^2 + p_2^2 = a^2$, for some constant a. It follows that

$$p_1^2 + p_2^2 = p_1^2 + r^2 p_1^2 = p_1^2(1 + r^2) = a^2,$$

and so $p_1 = a/(1+r^2)^{1/2}$. All this is now put together to obtain $r' = (p_2/p_1)' = p_2'/p_1 - p_2 p_1'/p_1^2 = g(r)(1+r^2)/p_1 = g(r)(1+r^2)^{3/2}/a$. Hence:

$$r' = g(r)\frac{(1+r^2)^{3/2}}{a}. \tag{4.7}$$

The sign of r' depends on the sign of $g(r)$. One now shows that $g(r)$ has at least one positive root, which is an attractor, or, if there are multiple roots, all solutions tend to one of these equilibria. In either case, the market is stable (Exercise 4.6.8). The key to seeing this is the fact that Eq.(4.7) is a scalar equation and it therefore suffices to look at the sign of the derivative r'. For example, if $g(r)$ has the form shown in Fig. 4.5, then each of the outside equilibria is an attractor, as we explained in the previous section, and all solutions tend to either one or the other.

4.4. A Catastrophe Model of Fishing

It appears that sardines and similar species of fish have a difficult time breeding at low population densities and their survival is enhanced with increasing density, up to a level at which overcrowding begins to have an inhibitory effect on reproduction. This is achieved by swimming in *schools*, large and closely packed swarms, since this confers more protection from predators. Unlike some other species that follow a logistic per capita growth rate $r(1 - x/K)$, which decreases linearly with an increase in density x, the per capita growth rate of sardines is probably better modeled by a term that begins low and increases with x for awhile before decreasing. This would reflect an initially low growth rate that increases with population density x and then declines when x is large. A simple example of this is the function $rx(1 - x/k)$.

Consider now a fishing zone with unrestricted access. Any number of fishermen, with their trawlers and nets and, in recent years, electronic fish detectors, can harvest the fish. Let E be the total fishing effort in terms of the vessels and fishing gear, as well as manpower deployed per unit time, and let ν denote the fraction of each ton of fish that is caught per unit effort. Then νEx is the total catch per unit time, where x is the fish density in the fixed zone, measured in tons. An increase in E signifies that the fishing effort has intensified. If we adopt the per capita reproduction rate of schooling fish, then the rate of change of x is given by

$$x' = rx^2\left(1 - \frac{x}{K}\right) - \nu Ex, \tag{4.8}$$

where the second term on the right reflects the loss due to fishing. We note, parenthetically, that if the per capita reproduction rate decreases linearly with x, Eq.(4.8) becomes the logistic equation (4.4) that was described earlier.

Now we introduce some drastically simplified market economics. Suppose that the cost, in dollars, per unit effort is c and that p is the price obtained for the fish at the pier, in dollars per unit catch. The cost includes operating expenses as well as an amortized capital investment, while p reflects the market value of the fish. The net revenue from the harvest is proportional to $p\nu Ex - cE$. As long as this quantity is positive, the fishing effort increases. This follows from the idea that when a natural resource has unrestricted access, its exploitation continues unabated until the resource no longer provides any profit. In the case of a fishery, the harvesting would increase until the net revenue is zero or until the existing fish stock is exhausted. A fisherman who does not participate in the haul relinquishes his portion of the take to his competitors. A sole owner of the fishery might want to harvest less relentlessly, since a prematurely depleted fishery does him no good, and he has the incentive to balance a short-term gain from aggressive fishing against the potential long-term benefits of gradual exploitation; but in an open access fishery, the short-term myopic view prevails that as long as a profit is to be made, there is no reason to incur a loss by not joining the scramble for what is left.

Of course, this is a gross simplification, since no fishery is totally unregulated, and as fish stocks begin to be depleted, a conservationist attitude becomes more prevalent among the regulating agencies. Moreover, as competition intensifies for a dwindling resource, the effort must necessarily increase, which would discourage those fishermen who have alternative employment opportunities. Nevertheless, we adopt this somewhat fictional view and write an equation for the rate of change of fishing effort as

$$E' = \alpha E(p\nu x - c) \tag{4.9}$$

This says that E increases or decreases at a rate proportional to the net revenue. If the net profit is positive, it increases; otherwise, it decreases. The constant of proportionality is generally small to reflect the fact that there is a certain inertia in the way the fishing industry responds to a perceived change in either market conditions or in the availability of fish in the ocean. It takes some time to hire or lay off personnel, invest in new gear, or put additional boats out to sea. These changes take place at a smaller pace than the breeding of fish. For this reason, E is considered to be a *slow variable* relative to x, which is deemed to be *fast*.

At this juncture, we need to modify Eq.(4.9) by adjoining a small constant e:

$$x' = e + rx^2\left(1 - \frac{x}{K}\right) - \nu Ex. \tag{4.10}$$

The interpretation of this is that even when the observable population density x is zero, some additional fish are spawned because a few members of the species found a refuge, or because additional fish migrate into the fishing zone at some constant rate. We are considering a threshold effect here that just barely allows for the possibility of recovery. It also embodies the idea that when fish stocks are sufficiently reduced, further exploitation ceases either because it is not worth the effort or because a regulatory agency has imposed a ban.

Our fishery model consists of the coupled equations (4.9) and (4.10), which is of the form (4.1) except that we prefer to label our variables as x and E instead of x_1 and x_2.

We begin the discussion by temporarily fixing E at some given value. Then Eq.(4.10) has either one or three equilibria, depending on the value of E, which are obtained by setting x' to zero. This occurs at the intersection of the curve $g(x) = e + rx^2(1 - x/K)$ with the line defined by $h(x) = \nu Ex$ in the x, E plane. This is illustrated in Figs. 4.6 through 4.10.

By examining the sign of x', we can determine the stability properties of the equilibria, as explained in Section 4.2. A single equilibrium is always an attractor, but if one has three equilibria, the middle one is always unstable. These results follow from the fact that x increases or decreases according to whether $h(x)$ is less or greater than $g(x)$.

Since E varies slowly with respect to x (recall that α is a small constant), it follows that x responds quickly to a change in E and so it resides at or near its closest attractor. This means that a study of the pair of equations for x and E can be simplified considerably by letting E be a gradually changing parameter in the single equation for x.

Consider now the following scenario. Initially, the fishing effort is slight, e.g., E_a, and so a single equilibrium occurs at a high value of x, indicated by x_a in Fig. 4.6. This is an attractor, as we already

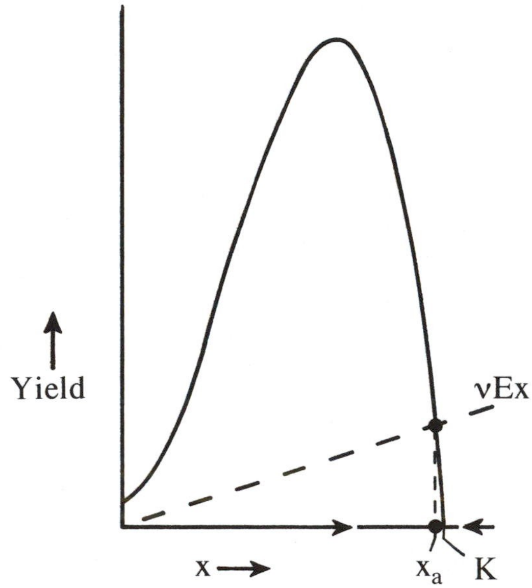

Figure 4.6. Fish harvesting at level $E = .17$ gives an attractor at a high population level. This is an asymptotically stable equilibrium of Eq. (4.8). Here, and in the next four figures, the straight line has slope E and $k = 6, e = .3, r = 1$, and $\nu = 1$.

noted, and so the fish stock is x_a when fishing effort is E_a. An increase in E to E_b reduces the equilibrium to x_b, but even though x is now less, the total yield νEx is greater. Note that as E increases, there is a value at which the straight line is tangent to the curve (Fig. 4.7). This is called a *bifurcation point*, since two new equilibria are created for all E that are just beyond this point of tangency. So there are now three equilibria when $E = E_b$, but the middle one is unstable, and since x moves quickly to the nearest attractor, the fish density remains at x_b and does not move to the other attractor at $x_{b'}$ (Fig. 4.8).

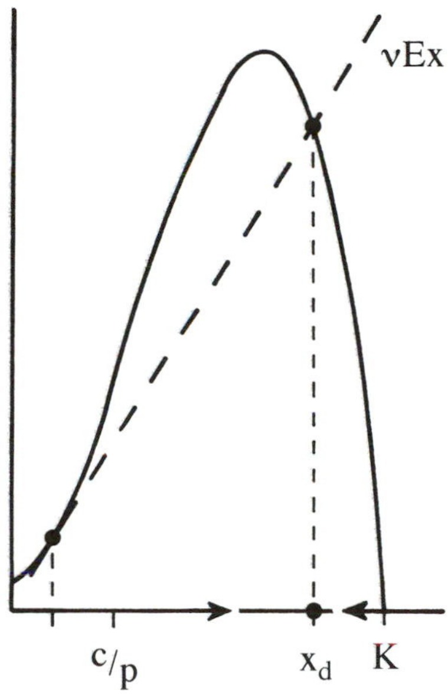

Figure 4.7. $E = 1$, and at this value two new equilibria emerge just as the line becomes tangent to the curve. This value of E is called a *bifurcation point.*

The maximum sustainable yield occurs at a level of fishing effort where fish density is x_m, namely, at the maximum of $g(x)$. Beyond that, the fish stocks decline and prices begin to rise through scarcity. Ironically, this can draw new entrants into the fishery and the competition to catch intensifies. The line defined by $h(x)$ is tangent to the curve $g(x)$ at x_t, as we see in Fig. 4.9. Assume for now that the cost-to-price ratio c/p is less than x_t. As E increases further, we enter a phase of biological overfishing, since immature fish begin to be captured before they can breed, and eventually, when the point of tangency at x_t is attained, there is another bifurcation at which two of the equilibria coalesce and disappear, leaving a single equilibrium

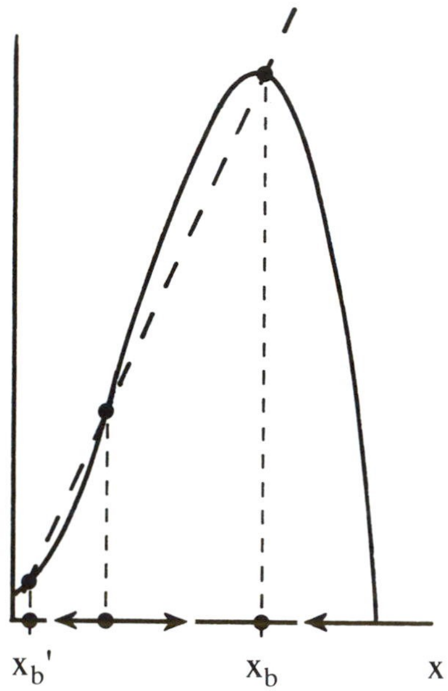

Figure 4.8. Three equilibria when $E = 1.3$. Two of these are attractors and the middle point is a repeller.

at a much lower fish density x_c. This is an attractor, and so the fish stocks suddenly fall to this new equilibrium, an event that signifies the collapse of the fishery (Fig. 4.10). Because x_c is below the ratio c/p, we see from Eq.(4.9) that E' is now negative, and so fishing effort reverses itself. In effect, it no longer pays to go out to sea, and many trawlers begin to rust in the harbor.

A dramatic example of such a collapse is provided by the Peruvian anchovy fishery. Using the number of vessels deployed per unit time as a measure of effort, the actual catch (in 10^6 tons) is given in Table. 4.1. As E increased from 1963, so did the catch, but by 1973 the yield had fallen to pre-1959 levels.

Table 4.1.

Year	Effort	Yield
1959	1.4	1.91
1964	5.8	8.86
1968	8.9	10.26
1973	46.5	1.78

Eventually, recovery of the fish stocks takes place because of reduced harvesting. As x increases, the line eventually becomes tangent to the lower hump of the curve (Fig. 4.7), which again is a bifurcation point at which two equilibria coalesce. Beyond this, there is only one attractor, at the relatively high value of x_d. The fish density, therefore, makes a sudden resurgence at a level that exceeds c/p, where the derivative of E is once again positive. Some ships feel encouraged to go out to sea and the process starts over again, leading to a cyclic boom and bust population dynamics in which a sort of hysteresis effect takes place, since the path to recovery follows a different route than the path to collapse (Fig. 4.11). When Eqs. (4.9) and (4.10) are considered simultaneously as a pair, the nullcline method that was explained in the preceding sections suggests that a closed cycle does indeed exist in the x, E plane (Exercise 4.6.5).

Models in which rapid jumps take place from one plateau to another as a certain parameter crosses a bifurcation point form part of *catastrophe theory*, which explains the title of this section. Note that if the constant e is zero, the population crashes to zero and becomes extinct. On the other hand, if the per capita growth is logistic, so that Eq.(4.8) is replaced by Eq.(4.4), then a quite different dynamic takes place in which x is asymptotically stable at the value of c/p. This can be demonstrated in a similar way, and there is no need to repeat the nearly identical arguments here.

We have attributed a crash in fish density to overfishing. There could also be unfavorable climatic changes that restrict the rate at which fish larvae develop into young adults. This corresponds to a decrease in the rate constant r. These are called recruitment fail-

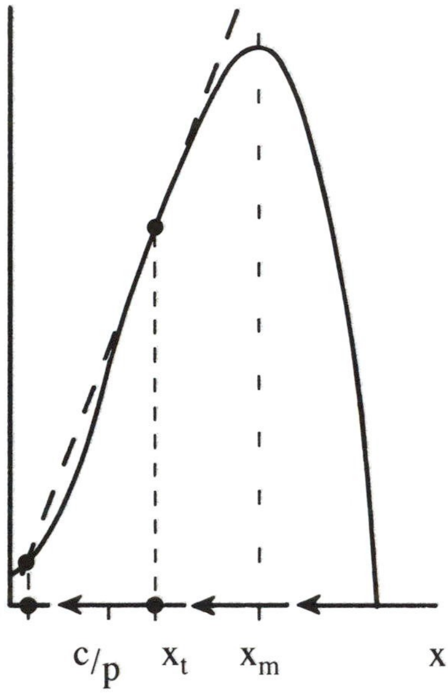

Figure 4.9. Two equilibria coalesce into one when the line is again tangent to the curve. This occurs at $E = 1.6$.

ures and an already seriously depleted fishery is especially prone to collapse when such an environmental fluctuation occurs. Moreover, a diminished species can be replaced by other, commercially uninteresting species, and these may inhibit the recovery of the original fishery. We saw how this can happen in the preceding section, when one of two strongly competing species drives the other to extinction as we move from one basin of attraction to another.

The model assumes that there is no seasonal preference for hatching and that reproduction is unaffected by age and sex differences. In spite of these and similar simplifications, that model appears to mimic the gross behavior of certain types of fisheries, such as an-

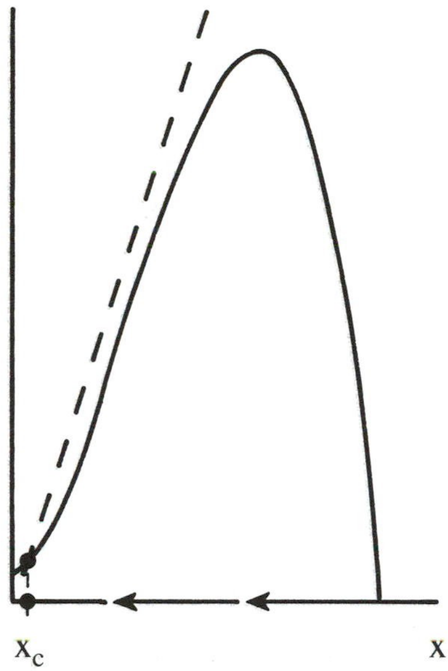

Figure 4.10. There is a single attractor at a low value of population when $E = 1.8$.

chovies and sardines, in which excessive exploitation can lead to a sudden collapse followed by gradual recovery.

If the cost-to-price ratio c/p increases to a level beyond x_m, the fishery avoids a crash (Exercise 4.6.4). This can be ensured by governmental intervention in the form of imposing a tax T per unit catch. This effectively reduces the net price for the fish to $p-T$, and if the tax is severe enough, $c/(p-T)$ will indeed exceed x_m. There are other regulations that can and are imposed on fisheries, especially after a disastrous failure, such as catch quotas, licenses and fees that restrict the entry of additional fishermen, and no fishing zones. These are not considered here.

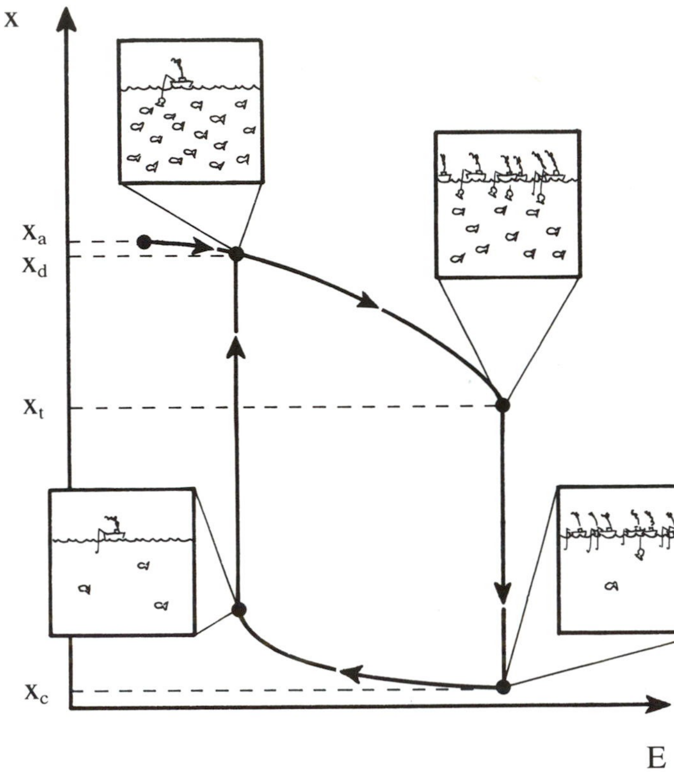

Figure 4.11. A curve showing the change in population x as fishing effort varies. The decline in x follows a different path than its recovery, a phenomenon known as *hysteresis*.

4.5. Measles Epidemics

Our intention is to model childhood epidemics such as measles, chicken pox, and mumps in order to track the dynamics of outbreaks of these contagious diseases.

We begin by dividing the population of a given region into four categories: *Susceptibles* are those individuals who are able to contract the communicable disease, *exposed* are infected people who are not yet able to transmit the disease to others, *infectives* are those who are capable of spreading the disease, and *recovered*.

With childhood illnesses, it is largely true that a recovered person becomes permanently immune, and so the last category includes individuals who are immune to begin with. Denote the fractions of susceptible, exposed, infective, and recovered in the population by S, E, I, R, respectively. We assume that all newborns are susceptibles at birth, and that the population size remains constant by balancing births, on one hand, with deaths and emigration on the other.

Let r be the average birth rate ($1/r$ is therefore the average life expectancy), and b the contact rate, which is the average fraction of susceptibles contracted by a single infective. The disease is transmitted in proportion to the number of possible encounters between infectives and susceptibles, and so

$$S' = r - rS - bSI \tag{4.11}$$

models the rate of change of S. The second term on the right expresses the fact that, since population is constant, susceptibles are removed by death and emigration at the same rate r that they enter the population.

The class of exposed individuals increases over time at a rate equal to the rate at which susceptibles become infected, namely, bSI. They disappear from the population at a rate rE, due to death and emigration, and at a rate aE, where a is the average number of exposed people that become contagious per unit time. The reciprocal $1/a$ is, therefore, the mean latency period during which the disease incubates prior to becoming infectious. Putting this together gives the equation

$$E' = bSI - rE - aE. \tag{4.12}$$

The infectives are now seen to increase at a rate aE and to be removed at rates rI (for the same reason as before) and cI, where c is the average number of infected people that recover per unit time; the reciprocal $1/c$ is then the mean infectious period. Thus,

$$I' = aE - rI - cI. \tag{4.13}$$

Finally, the recovered class evidently increases at a rate cI and disappears at rate rR:

$$R' = cI - rR. \tag{4.14}$$

The four coupled equations describe the epidemic model but are too formidable to handle using the tools at our disposal. To get some idea of the behavior of the solution to this system, we simplify a bit and ignore the class E by assuming that the latency period is zero. This means that susceptibles are immediately infected, and so Eq.(4.13) for I needs to be replaced by

$$I' = bSI - rI - cI.$$

Three equations remain:

$$\begin{aligned} S' &= r - rS - bSI, \\ I' &= bSI - rI - cI, \\ R' &= cI - rR. \end{aligned} \tag{4.15}$$

The first two equations are independent of R, and so we can simplify further by retaining only these two. Since $S + I + R = 1$, the value of R is obtained from a knowledge of S and I. Thus,

$$\begin{aligned} S' &= r(1 - S) - bSI, \\ I' &= I(bS - (r + c)). \end{aligned} \tag{4.16}$$

Using the heuristic nullcline approach described in Section 4.2 (with details worked out in Exercise 4.6.5) we surmise that there are oscillatory solutions about the equilibrium state defined by

$$S = (r + c)/b, \quad I = r(b - r - c)/b(r + c).$$

The quantity $(r+c)/b$ is taken to be less than one in order to guarantee that I is positive at the equilibrium. This is called the *threshold effect*, since it asserts that the total population in the region must be large enough for a disease to become endemic: The population consists of the fractions of S, I, and R, which add to unity, and this must exceed $(r + c)/b$. Therefore, if the ratio of the recovery rate c to the contact rate b is small enough, the epidemic can be sustained. This implies that intervention on the part of public health officials can have an impact on the severity or even the likelihood of an epidemic. For example, inoculation of schoolchildren reduces the number of susceptibles, while quick isolation of infectives increases the removal rate c.

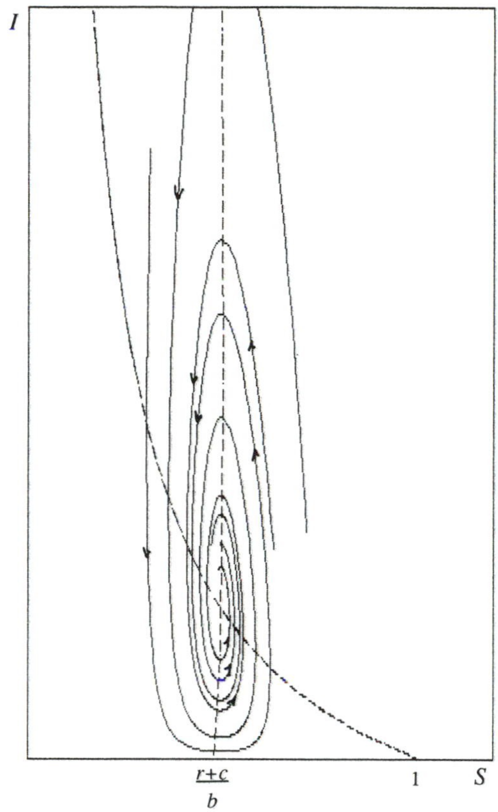

Figure 4.12. Trajectories for the epidemic equations in (4.16).

We note parenthetically that when $r = 0$ (total population remains constant), the threshold level c/b has a somewhat different interpretation (Exercise 4.6.9).

The trajectories for a typical case are shown in Fig. 4.12, and we observe that the oscillations wind down to a point attractor as the number of infectives waxes and wanes. A numerical integration of the full set of Eqs.(4.11)–(4.14) reveals a similar pattern of damped oscillations, which appears to indicate a cyclic recurrence of outbreaks with diminishing severity; but the actual data on measles shows a different pattern in which the disease recurs with levels of severity that fluctuate erratically from year to year. In New York City, for

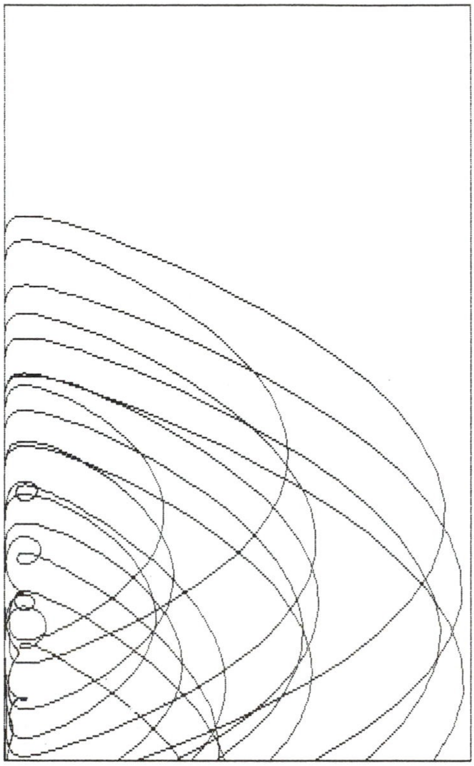

Figure 4.13. Projection onto the I, R plane of the attractor of periodically forced epidemic equations.

example, measles outbreaks from 1928 to 1963 (when large-scale vaccination of schoolchildren began), the monthly data on measles cases exhibits peaks and troughs that seem to vary unpredictably.

There are several possible reasons for the discrepancy between what the model predicts and what one observes. The most compelling, perhaps, is that the parameter b, the rate at which the disease is transmitted, need not be constant and can in fact vary widely. The disease pathogen appears to be more virulent during winter months, at a time when children are confined together in school; contact is less frequent and not as close during the summer months. With this in mind the parameter b is replaced in the model by a periodic function having a period of one year, with a low value in July and a high one in February:

$$b(t) = b_0(1 + b_1 \cos 2\pi t),$$

where b_0 is the average contact rate and b_1, a number between zero and one, measures the magnitude of the seasonal effect. The time $t = 0$ represents the beginning of February. With $b(t)$ substituted into Eq.(4.11), the original model can be integrated numerically to give solutions that indeed mimic the data seen in New York City and elsewhere for actual measles outbreaks. In certain parameter regimes, in fact, the periodically forced solutions are indistinguishable from random fluctuations, a phenomenon that some authors describe as a manifestation of *chaotic dynamics*, in which, loosely speaking, the trajectories settle down to a complicated attractor in state space that is neither a point nor a cycle. Motion on the attractor appears haphazard, as we see in Fig. 4.13, which is a projection onto the I, R plane of the solutions in four-dimensional S, E, I, R space. Here, the trajectories loop back and forth irregularly, always hugging the vertical axis on each return. Note that although the solutions appear to tangle, this is not a violation of the uniqueness principle because what is being viewed here is merely a two-dimensional projection of nonintersecting trajectories in higher-dimensional space.

Figure 4.14 shows the fraction I of infective cases over a 30-year period as obtained from an integration of the periodically forced equations (4.11)–(4.14). The parameters in the model are estimated from census data and medical records as $r = .02$ per year, $b_0 = 1,800$ per year, $a = 35.58$ per year, $c = 100$ per year, and $b_1 = .285$, as reported in the work of Olsen and Schaeffer that is mentioned in Section 4.7. The severity of the outbreaks varies erratically from year to year and resembles that found in the actual New York City data from 1928 to 1963, during which the epidemic peaked at about 25,000 cases a year. With a total population of about 6 million, this corresponds to a maximum I of roughly .004, as shown in Fig. 4.14.

Another manifestation of chaotic dynamics is extreme sensitivity to initial conditions. Small changes in inital values of any of the variables produce solutions that rapidly diverge from each other over

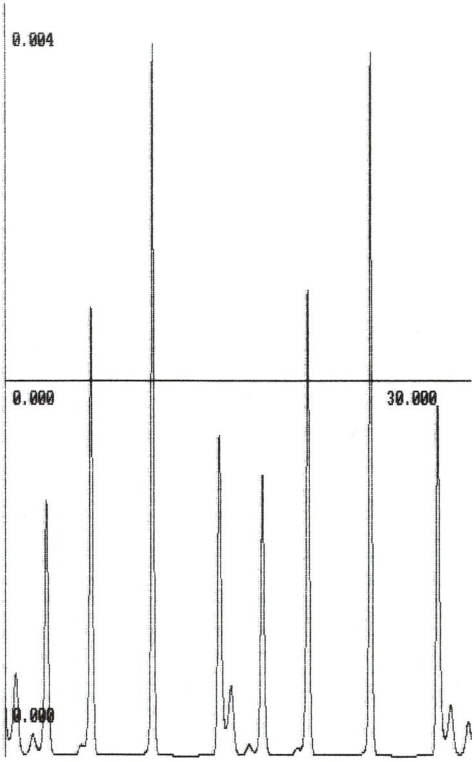

Figure 4.14. Infectives over a 30-year period from the model equations (4.9)–(4.12), with model parameters estimated from census data and medical records as $r = .02, b_0 = 1800$, $b_1 = .285, a = 35.58, c = 100$.

time. To illustrate this, we change the initial value of S by only .001 from the value used to obtain Fig. 4.14. All other initial values, for I, E, and R, remain the same. The result is shown in Fig. 4.15, where we see that the solution remains roughly the same for a while to the one shown in the previous figure, but soon it changes dramatically so that by the time 30 years have elapsed, the value of I is evolving along a completely different part of the attractor. This shows that we can never hope to replicate exactly the actual dynamics of a chaotic process, and the solutions only illustrate what the typical behavior is like. These numerical results are somewhat

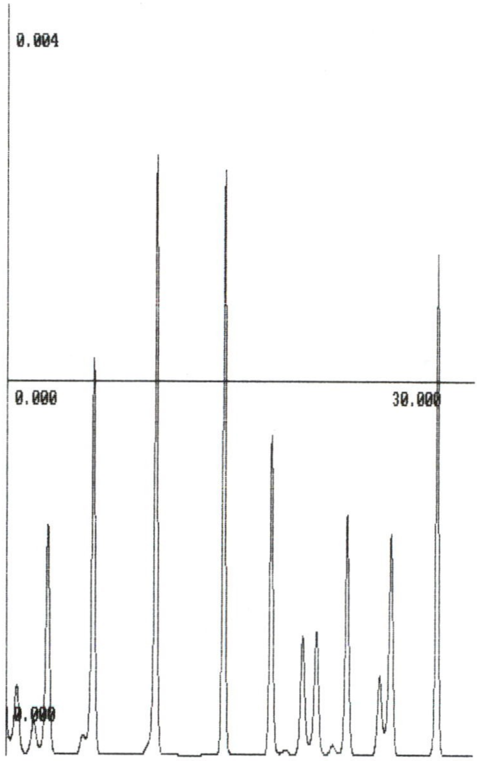

Figure 4.15. Infectives over a 30-year period from the periodically forced model equations (4.11)–(4.14) with the initial condition for the variable S differing by .001 from the value used to obtain Fig. 4.14, with $b_1 = .285$.

unsatisfactory, however, since the actual New York City data from 1945 onward manifests alternating highs and lows in the number of reported cases of measles, with a severe outbreak in one year followed by a mild incidence of disease in the subsequent year. The problem is that the parameter b_1 that measures the effect of seasonality is not known exactly, and even a slight change in its value can have a notable effect in the computational results. For example, a change to $b_1 = .275$ gives alternating biannual peaks in the number of cases, as shown in Fig. 4.16, which is more consistent with the data from 1945 onward, but on the other hand, does not reach the reported levels of

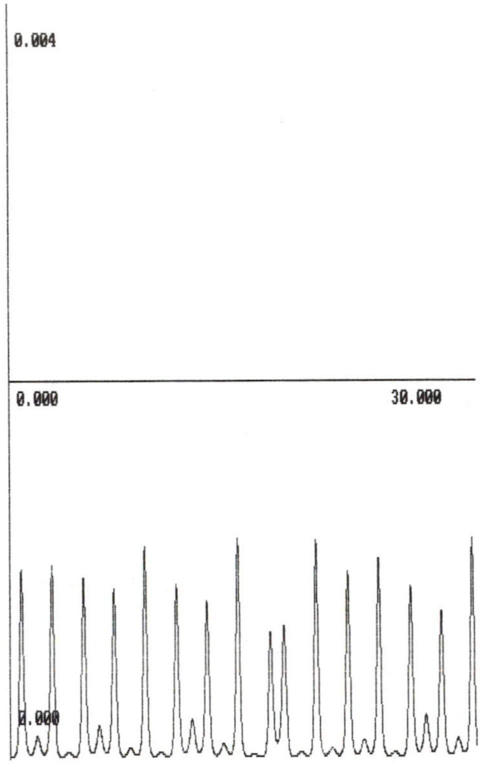

Figure 4.16. Infectives over a 30-year period from the periodically forced model equations (4.11)–(4.14), with $b_1 = .275$.

severity that were visable in Figs. 4.14 and 4.15, where $b_1 = .285$.

Although the model is a plausible caricature of the actual dynamics of a recurrent epidemic, it is at least arguable whether or not an alternative formulation would be more convincing: for example, allowing the parameters to vary at random to represent chance variations, such as the wayward movement of infectives into and out of the region. One can also try stochastic models in which infectiousness, transmission, and latency periods all follow probability distributions. This was hinted at, for the case of smallpox, in Exercises 3.6.9 and 3.6.10.

These and similar models of epidemics are of considerable interest for the insight they provide into how actual diseases can spread in a population not only over time, as we discussed here, but also in space (Exercise 5.4.5). Moreover, they fit into a general class of models in which species interact competitively or through dominance at a rate that is proportional to the product of their population densities. In the present instance, the species include S and I, but they could also be different chemicals whose molecules collide, or algae and their plankton grazers in a marine trophic system, or even hostile factions of humans during warfare (Exercises 4.6.2. 4.6.6, and 4.6.7).

4.6. Exercises

4.6.1. Solve Eq.(4.4) using the method of separation of variables (which is discussed in Chapter 2, Section 3, of the book by Redheffer [25] listed in the references). Sketch the solution curves and verify that they tend to $K(1 - E/r)$.

4.6.2. Two chemical species a and b interact to form a chemical compound c. The formation of c occurs at a rate proportional to the product of the concentrations of a and b. Moreover, c itself can break apart into its constituents a and b at a rate proportional to its own concentration. Initially, c is zero, but a and b have identical nonzero concentrations $a_0 = b_0$. There is a conservation law in effect that says that the total amount of a is preserved, which implies that at any time t the amount of a locked up in c plus the free amount of unused a is constant. The same is true for b. In effect, this states that a or b each lose a molecule at the same rate that a molecule of c is formed.

Write down a differential equation model for the formation of c, and, using the methods of Section 4.2, deduce the properties of its solution.

4.6.3. Do a nullcline analysis on model (4.5) for the case $r/a > L$, $s/b > K$. What does this suggest about the nontrivial equilibrium?

4.6.4. In the fishery model of Section 4.4, suppose that $c/p > x_m$, and show that the equilibrium is asymptotically stable by looking at the sign of the derivative of x, as in the text. Verify the result by employing Lemma 4.1.

4.6.5. Use the nullcline approach on Eqs. (4.16) to deduce oscillatory behavior of the solutions about the equilibrium.

4.6.6. A simple model of a marine trophic system consists of a microscopic species of algae that is cropped by a larger species of herbivorous plankton that graze on the algae. Let x be the density of algae and suppose that the growth rate of x is logistic. The effect of cropping by the predatory plankton diminishes the overall growth at an insignificant rate when x is very small, and although its effect is more pronounced as x grows, the rate of predation becomes proportional to a term that saturates at a finite value. The interpretation of this is that when the algae is scarce, the predator feeds on other marine plant life, and even though it devotes more attention to the algae species when it becomes abundant, eventually its appetite is satiated and cropping occurs at a constant rate, independent of the density of x. An example of such a predation term is $bx^2/(1+x^2)$. Putting these terms together gives the model

$$x' = rx\left(1 - \frac{x}{K}\right) - \frac{bx^2}{(1+x^2)}.$$

The parameter r is allowed to vary slowly up and down to represent gradual shifts in environmental factors that affect the growth rate of the algae, such as a change in water temperature as we move from the winter season to summer. Depending on r, show that there are either one or three equilibria, and assume that growth in x is fast in comparison to the environment. This means that the algae adapt quickly to small changes in climate. Using an argument similar to that used in Section 4.4, discuss the possibilities of a catastrophic change in the density of x as certain thresholds in r are reached. A sudden surge in algae population is known as a *bloom*, and what the model shows is that a rapid jump upwards to bloom conditions can be followed by a sudden crash to low population levels as environmental conditions become unfavorable, but the jump downward follows a different path. This is the phenomenon of hysteresis discussed earlier.

4.6.7. Two enemy forces engage in guerilla warfare in which they kill each other at rates proportional to the number of troops on the opposite side of the conflict. This is a reasonable assumption in conventional combat, in which firepower increases as the enemy troop size grows. The rates need not be equal, since one force may be more effective than the other. Model this by a pair of equations and show, depending on the initial troop sizes, that one side or the other will be eliminated in finite time. This is the simplest form of what is known as a *combat model.* How would you modify the equations in the event that one of the two sides suffered casualties from self-inflicted wounds at a rate proportional to the number of troops remaining ?

4.6.8. Show that the equation $r' = g(r)(1 + r^2)^{3/2}/a$ has at least one root for $r > 0$. If it the only root, establish that it is an attractor. When there are multiple roots, all solutions will tend to one of them or the other. Interpret this in terms of the two goods market example discussed in Section 4.3 by showing that all prices tend to an attractor, that establishes that the market is stable. *Hint: If* $g(r) = 0$ *for some* r *and if* p_2 *and* p_1 *are two prices whose ratio* *is this value of r, then they define a vector* $\mathbf{q}$ *for which*

$$f(\mathbf{q}) = \begin{pmatrix} -rg(r) \\ g(r) \end{pmatrix} = 0.$$

4.6.9 Equations (4.16) can be simplified further by ignoring the birth rate r. This supposes that the population size is fixed with no new recruits or defections during the period of an epidemic, which is a reasonable assumption for diseases of short duration. the equations now read as

$$\begin{aligned} S' &= -bSI, \\ I' &= bSI - cI. \end{aligned} \tag{4.17}$$

The fraction R of recovered individuals is initially zero and, since $S + I + R = 1$, this means that $S + I = 1$ at $t = 0$. From the chain rule of differentiation, one obtains, for all S, I in the positive quadrant,

$$dI/ds = \frac{I'}{S'} = -1 + \frac{c}{bS}.$$

Integrating both sides of this relation with respect to S yields

$$I(t) = -S(t) + \left(\frac{c}{b}\right) \ln S(t) + \text{constant}. \tag{4.18}$$

Assume that $c/b < 1$. Plot the solution curves in the S, I plane and interpret the results in light of the discussion in Section 4.5. Show, in particular, that if S is initially greater than c/b, there is an epidemic, after some infectives are introduced into the population, whereas if S begins at some value less than c/b, the disease does not take root and the infectives diminish over time. This is the threshold condition. In any case, show that the epidemic dies out not for any lack of susceptibles in the population, but rather because there are no more infectives.

4.7. Further Readings

The models discussed in this chapter have their origins in a literature going back many decades and are, by now, classical. The exploitation of renewable resources and, in particular, fish harvesting models are discussed in the book by Clark [19], while epidemic models are the subject of another book [20]. An excellent introduction to models of interacting populations, including combat among opposing armies, is to be found in the collection of essays edited by Braun *et al.* [22]. Competition in a market economy, a topic we touched on in Section 4.3, is based on the papers listed in [23]. The hypothesis of market equilibrium is, of course, questionable, since a real economy is never closed and the individuals involved do not always behave rationally, as we suppose here. Nevertheless, the model remains a useful paradigm of an ideal market place.

A highly recommended discussion of differential equation modeling is in a little booklet by Tuchinsky, [24], where the interaction between an insect, the spruce budworm, and the forests it defoliates, is treated in a most instructive manner. At the same time, it provides an introduction to catastrophe models, a topic we alluded to in Section 4.4.

The necessary background in differential equations can be acquired from the lucid book by Redheffer [25], but since we also rely on numerically computed solutions, it would be useful to have available a software package for PC use that displays the solutions graphically, as we occasionally do in the text. Two friendly packages that can be used in a DOS operating environment are listed in references [30] and [31].

After the vaccination of schoolchildren began in earnest in many communities around 1963, the incidence of measles declined significantly, only to reappear among preschoolers during the late 1980s. (See, for example, "Resurgence of measles prompts new recommendations on vaccination," *New York Times*, Jan. 11, 1990.) The idea that some recurrent epidemics may be a manifestation of chaotic dynamics is based on the article by Olsen and Schaeffer [26] and is reviewed in a short article by Pool [27]. An elementary introduction to chaotic attractors is to be found in reference [28].

The notion that a renewable resource such as a fishery, forest, or grazing lands, which are open to exploitation to all without restriction, will ultimately be devastated in the stampede to exploit it in one's own interest, without regard to the common good, has been called "the tragedy of the commons" in an elegant article by Garrett Hardin [29].

The fishery problem continues to resurface (for example, see "Northwest fishermen catch everything, and that's a problem," *New York Times*, Nov. 13, 1988), and so models like the one discussed in Section 4.3 remain appealing even if they are admittedly too simple.

We cannot resist quoting a few lines from Dr. Seuss's book *On Beyond Zebra* (Geisel, 1955), in which he talks about creatures called nutches who are in competition with each other. The quote is especially apt in view of the discussion in Section 4.2:

> These nutches have troubles, the biggest of which is
> The fact that there are many more Nutches than Nitches.
> Each Nutch in a Nitch knows that some other Nutch
> Would like to move into his Nitch very much.
> So each Nutch in a Nitch has to watch that small Nitch
> Or Nutches who haven't got Nitches will snitch.

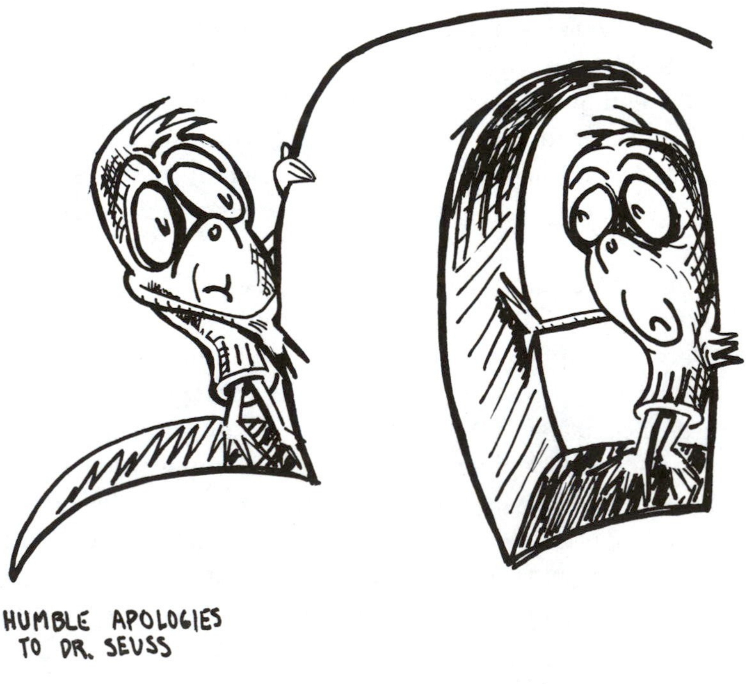

5

Algae Blooms, Pollution, and Squirrels

5.1. Background

On a day in late spring, one begins to notice patches of discolored water in the bay, dark brown like mud. A few days later, the patches have spread, and after several more weeks tangled masses of seaweed litter the beaches. The bay fishermen complain about the poor harvest of shellfish. Elsewhere, large patches of red appear off the coast, further out at sea, and thousands of dead fish pile up on the coastline.

This may appear to be the opening scene of a science fiction movie, but in fact it is the stuff of a commonplace occurrence worldwide, year after year. The red, brown, and green splotches are dense accumulations of microscopic algae that in one way or other are toxic to the marine life around them.These algae *blooms* find conditions in the lakes, estuaries, and off shore waters propitious for unimpeded and rapid growth until their large numbers begin to act as a brake and millions die off, leaving in their wake oxygen-starved waters as the cells decay.

Although something of the temporal dynamics of these blooms is beginning to be understood, our concern will only be with the spatial distribution of these cell masses. The interplay between reproduction of algae by cell division and their dispersion in the turbulent waters sets a lower bound on the size of these plankton patches, a topic that will be taken up in Section 5.3.

One reason for the anomalous growth of algae is the nutrient enrichment of coastal waters as a result of wastewater that is contaminated with fecal matter, detergents, and fertilizers, and then discharged into bays and inlets through sewage outfalls, or as runoff from paved surfaces and farmlands adjacent to the shoreline. The organic pollutants will decompose in the water through bacterial action. This process of metabolization, called *eutrophication*, reduces the amount of oxygen dissolved in the water, a condition that can be hazardous to both fish and man.

The Federal Water Pollution Control Act of 1972 was intended to deflect the impact of regional growth on the degradation of coastal waters by requiring shoreline regions to prepare plans for the protection of these natural resources. To do this, however, one needs to estimate how waste discharges affect water quality. This is discussed in a simplified setting in Section 5.5.

A few *killer bees*, a species originally imported from Africa, were accidently released in Brazil in recent times; they began to colonize portions of South and Central America by migrating in swarms and, by now, they have reached our border. In the last century, some captive gypsy moth larvae escaped in Massachusetts and spread over the northeastern states. The proliferation of both these insects over wide-ranging areas has been a cause of distress to many.

A similar event took place around the turn of the century when the American gray squirrel, *Sciurus carolinensis*, was released into the English countryside, where it spread to colonize much of the habitat formerly occupied by the indigenous red squirrel, *Sciurus vulgaris*. The influx of the gray squirrel has coincided with the decline and disappearance of its red relative, and although there may be several reasons for this decline, such as disease and environmental changes, a most plausible hypothesis is that it has been outcompeted by the larger gray squirrel, which is also known to be a more prolific breeder. It is likely that a substantial overlap in the niches of these two species has favored the advance of the grays over the reds. The interplay between competition and dispersion gives rise to interesting wave-like patterns of squirrel densities in space that are in rough agreement with those actually seen in England and Wales. This idea is explored in Section 5.6.

Another example of wave-like spatial dispersion occurs in the spread of some diseases. The epidemic model that was considered in the previous chapter can be extended to include the effect of a pathogen moving through a population of susceptibles. This is carried out in Exercise 5.7.5.

The mathematical apparatus necessary for these studies in diffusion is developed in the next section, where a certain partial differential equation is derived that connects dispersion in space to changes that take place over time.

5.2. Diffusion

When a bunch of particles collide, each is scattered at random, first in one direction and then another, in short back-and-forth excursions known as *molecular diffusion*. In addition to this ricocheting is the dispersal that takes place at large spatial scales due to the fact that the particles may be in a medium that is itself in haphazard motion. Algae cells in the ocean, for example, are subject to the vagaries of wind and tide. The cells are caught up in swirling eddies of a churning sea that tosses them to and fro. Although it may be a leap of the imagination to go from microscopic cells to animals, it is sometimes also appropriate to consider the dispersal of small mammals, such as squirrels as they migrate across fields and wooded glens, to be another form of diffusion, especially when to all appearances their motion is erratic and essentially unpredictable.

A simple model of diffusion on the one-dimensional x axis is a random walk. Let a particle make a series of short movements of length Δx, each of duration Δt, beginning at the origin. A move one step to the right takes place with probability p and one step to the left with probability $q, p+q=1$. Each move is assumed independent of the others, so we have a Markov chain of the type considered in

Chapter 1, in which the one-step transition probabilities are $p_{i,i+1} = p, p_{i,i-1} = q$, and $p_{i,j} = 0$ for all other i and j. The only difference in the present context is that the number of states is now infinite.

After n moves, the particle is at some position $x = r\Delta x$, where r is one of the integers, positive or negative. Let $u_{r,n}$ be the probability of being at x at time $t = n\Delta t$. The particle can reach x in one step from either the right or the left, and by conditioning on these disjoint events (see Appendix A), it follows that

$$u_{r,n+1} = pu_{r-1,n} + qu_{r+1,n}, \tag{5.1}$$

with $u_{0,0} = 1$ and $u_{r,0} = 0$ for $r \neq 0$.

We now assume that there is a continuous distribution of particles (cells or animals, in our case) whose concentration at position x and time t is some function $u(x,t)$. Of course, a bunch of discrete particles can never be smeared continuously across the axis, but for large numbers of particles, this is an acceptable fiction. If the integral of the density function u is normalized to unity on the x axis, then the probability of finding a particle between x and $x + \Delta x$ at time t is

$$\int_x^{x+\Delta x} u(s,t)ds. \tag{5.2}$$

The function u is taken to be smooth in the sense of possessing continuous partial derivatives of the second order in x and of the first order in t. Then, by Taylor's theorem in the calculus for functions of two variables, we obtain

$$u(x, t + \Delta t) = u(x,t) + u_t(x,t)\Delta t + o(\Delta t),$$

where $o(\Delta t)$ denotes terms of the order Δt^2 and higher, and u_t designates the partial derivative of u with respect to t. In a similar fashion, we also get

$$u(x + \Delta x, t) = u(x,t) + u_x(x,t)\Delta x + \frac{u_{xx}(x,t)\Delta x^2}{2} + o(\Delta x^2),$$

in which the subscripts indicate first and second partial derivatives with respect to x and the o term consists of quantities in Δx^3 and higher.

In order to put Eq.(5.1) to work for us, we employ a heuristic argument that is actually valid only in the limit as the step sizes go to zero. Suppose that Δt is very small. Then it is unlikely that a particle to the right or left of x at a distance Δx will change its direction during this brief interval, and so Eq.(5.1) can be written approximately as

$$u(x, t + \Delta t) = pu(x - \Delta x, t) + qu(x + \Delta x, t). \tag{5.3}$$

When $p > q$, there is a net drift to the right, as the particles move about at random. Therefore, we take p and q to equal $\frac{1}{2}$ to represent a walk without directional bias.

Substituting the Taylor expansion terms into Eq.(5.3) and dividing by Δt, it is easily seen that a number of terms cancel and what remains is

$$u_t = \frac{\Delta x^2}{2\Delta t} u_{xx} + \frac{o(\Delta t)}{\Delta t} + \frac{o(\Delta x^2)}{\Delta t}.$$

Now pass to the limit as Δt and Δx go to zero, in such a way that the ratio $\Delta x^2 / 2\Delta t$ remains equal to a constant; call it D. D is known as the *diffusion coefficient* and it measures the rate of spread of particles in units of distance squared per unit time. A large D indicates a higher degree of dispersion than one with a smaller value.

Keeping in mind that $o(\Delta t)/\Delta t$ goes to zero as $\Delta t \to 0$, we see that in the limit the preceding expression becomes

$$u_t = Du_{xx} \tag{5.4}$$

which is the diffusion equation. In the study of heat flow, where particles disperse by collisions, Eq.(5.4) is called the *heat equation.*

We now offer a second derivation of Eq.(5.4) using a new hypothesis about the mechanism of dispersion. As before, $u(x, t)$ is the concentration of particles of x at time t. Letting $q(x, t)$ be the net flow rate of particles in units of mass per unit time, we stipulate that the flow is proportional to the rate at which the concentration of particles varies in space, and that this takes place in the direction of decreasing concentration. What this says is that diffusion is more prominent in those regions where the concentration of the particles changes most rapidly, and that the ensuing motion tends to level the differences in density by causing the flow to move from high to low concentrations. Mathematically, this is expressed as

$$q = -cu_x \tag{5.5}$$

for some constant of proportionality c. This equation is sometimes called Fick's law of diffusion and, in the context of heat flow, as Newton's law of cooling. It is an empirical relation obtained from experimental observations.

The probability density $u(x,t)$ is measured as mass per unit distance. The total mass within an interval of length Δx is given by Eq.(5.2), and so the rate of change in mass within Δx at time t is the derivative of Eq.(5.2). This can be taken inside the integral sign to give

$$\int_x^{x+\Delta x} u_t(s,t)ds.$$

Now let $w(x,t)$ denote the net rate at which particles are added to the interval from external sources in units of density per unit time. The function w measures the net difference between sources and sinks and is assumed to be known. If w is positive, there is a net inflow of particles, with an outflow when it is negative. For example, algae reproduce by cell division and then die, and a simple expression for $w(x,t)$, in this case, is $ru(x,t)$, where the constant r is the net percapita difference between birth and death rates and u represents the concentration of cells. This assumes that the population density is not too large. (See, in this regard, the discussion in Section 4.2.)

At this point, one invokes the idea of *conservation of mass*, which stipulates that the total mass remains constant, accounting for all losses and gains. With this precept in mind, one requires that the rate of change in mass within Δx to equal the changes due to w within the same interval plus the difference in flow into and out of the boundary. The net flow into the interval at x is $q(x,t)$ and is $q(x+\Delta x,t)$ at the other end, and so, combining all the pieces of the flow, we find that

$$\int_x^{x+\Delta x} u_t(s,t)ds = q(x,t) - q(x+\Delta x,t) + \int_x^{x+\Delta x} w(s,t)ds.$$

By Taylor's theorem, again, this time for functions of a single variable, the terms in q may be written as $-q_x(x,t)\Delta x + o(\Delta x)$, where, as before, $o(\Delta x)$ are quantities that vanish faster than Δx. The same Taylor's theorem allows us to rewrite the integrals appearing in the preceding expression as $u_t(x,t)\Delta x + o(\Delta x)$ and $w(x,t)\Delta x + o(\Delta x)$, respectively. Dividing through by Δx, one gets

$$u_t = -qx + w + \frac{o(\Delta x)}{\Delta x},$$

and by letting Δx go to zero, one finds that

$$u_t = -q_x + w. \tag{5.6}$$

Using the fact that q is related to u through Eq.(5.5), we finally obtain the partial differential equation

$$u_t = cu_{xx} + w. \tag{5.7}$$

When there are no external sources or sinks, this reduces to the diffusion equation (5.4), provided that the constant c is equated to the diffusivity D. Thus, this derivation of the equation using a conservation of mass argument is consistent with the random walk hypothesis.

A different form of dispersion occurs when a substance of concentration u is constrained to move in a specific direction along the x axis as a result of being immersed in a medium that is itself in motion at some velocity v. This directional flow, called *advection*, is the opposite of random dispersion. An example would be the placement of a red dye, for example, into a river that is moving downstream in a specific direction. The meandering of the river as it makes its way to the sea is a curve whose arc length is measured along the scalar x axis. As will be seen later, the dye is a metaphor for a pollutant that is mixed in coastal waters that move seaward for awhile, and then reverse themselves, as a result of tidal motion.

In the case of advection, the flow rate q may be expressed as $q = vu$, in units of distance per unit time multiplied by mass per unit distance, namely, mass per unit time, where the velocity v is itself a function of x and t. Inserting this expression into conservation of mass equation (5.6), one gets

$$u_t = -(vu)_x + w, \tag{5.8}$$

which is known as the *advective equation.*

Note, for later use, that if motion takes place in a three-dimensional medium in which u changes only in the x direction, then u may be regarded as mass per unit volume by the simple expedient of dividing it by the cross-sectional area A of the medium, assumed to be constant. Equation (5.8) remains the same, but v must now be regarded as volume per unit time and w as volume density per unit time.

5.3. The Red Tide

Several species of algae form red patches in the sea when their concentrations increase. Outbreaks of these *red tides* have been observed in many parts of the globe, from the coastal waters of Japan to the Gulf of Mexico to the Adriatic Sea, and it is generally accepted that these patches are bodies of water that are especially favorable to the growth of the small plankton organisms. Conditions that contribute to this growth are an accumulation of stimulatory nutrients and levels of temperature and salinity that predispose the organisms to reproduce. These changes are brought about by a variety of causes, such as a storm episode that alters the composition of the water body or an upwelling of nutrients from deep layers of the sea. Tidal mixing and wind shears eventually break up the patches, but while they last the algae multiply rapidly. Outside the patches, conditions are less propitious to growth and an organism that is swept outside the patch boundary by the small-scale dispersive action of wind and wave is considered lost. There is an interplay, therefore, between the aggregative process of cell division and the anti-aggregative action of diffusion that carries the cells to waters that are physiologically unsuited to reproduction. Since growth takes place within the patch, it is proportional to surface area, while losses take place at the boundary and so are proportional to circumference. Therefore, as the area of the patch decreases, the effect of diffusion at the boundary becomes more significant, and eventually a limit is reached at which reproduction can no longer compensate for the losses. Thus, there must be a minimum patch size if a bloom is to form, and that is what we want to show next.

Algal cell reproduction is considered to be a source term that continuously adds to the population and is expressed in simplest form as $ru(x, y, t)$, where r is a constant percapita net growth rate and u is the concentration of algae at position x, y on the ocean surface at time t, so that ru is the growth rate in density. A more meticulous model of growth would be logistic, taking into account the inhibiting effect of overcrowding, but since there are continuous losses due to diffusion, the population is unlikely to reach a level that is self-limiting. In this regard, we suggest that reference be made to the discussion in Section 4.2.

The diffusion equation (5.7) is adopted as an appropriate model for dispersion with a source term $w = ru$. In the next section, our discussion will be extended to two spatial dimensions to account for planar motion on the surface of the sea, but the results obtained there do not differ in any significant way from those obtained from the simpler one-dimensional model. Our equation then is

$$u_t = Du_{xx} + ru. \tag{5.9}$$

We are not interested in actually solving Eq.(5.9). Our goal is merely to find a relationship between the parameters r and D and the patch width. To this end, we begin by reducing the partial differential equation to a pair of ordinary differential equations by guessing that the solution is of the form $u(x, t) = a(x)b(t)$ for suitable functions a and b. Whether this satisfies the equation or not remains to be seen. Make the substitution $u = ab$ into Eq.(5.9) and divide out by ab to get

$$\frac{b_t}{b} - r = \frac{Da_{xx}}{a}.$$

The left side of this relation is solely a function of t, while the right side depends only on x. Since these are independent variables, the only way both sides can equal each other for all x and t is for each to equal some constant c. After dividing by D, this gives us two separate equations:

$$\begin{aligned} b_t - (r + Dc)b &= 0, \\ a_{xx} - ca &= 0, \end{aligned} \tag{5.10}$$

in which the subscripts denote ordinary derivatives. Both these equations have solutions, and so the ploy of separating u in to a product of a and b is indeed workable. The first of these equations has the well-known solution $b(t) = b_0 \exp(r + Dc)t$, where b_0 is the value of b at the initial time $t = 0$. If c is positive, it shows that b increases at an exponential rate that exceeds $\exp(rt)$, which is the maximum growth rate that can be expected from cell divisions that take place at a rate ru, which is the stipulated growth in density per unit time. Therefore, for the model to be biologically reasonable, we must choose c to be negative. Define d to be the positive constant $-c$ so that

$$b(t) = b_0 \exp(r - Dd)t. \tag{5.11}$$

The second of the equations in (5.10) has the solutions $\cos(d^{1/2}x)$ and $\sin(d^{1/2}x)$, as one verifies by substitution. A linear combination of these two functions is also a solution (see Appendix B), and we write

$$a(x) = c_1 \cos(d^{1/2}x) + c_2 \sin(d^{1/2}x). \tag{5.12}$$

At this point, we must model the effect of the patch boundary. Suppose that the two ends of the patch occur at positions 0 and L. We impose the conditions that u be zero at $x = 0$ and $x = L$ for all t to capture the notion that the waters are inhospitable to growth outside the patch. When x is zero, the expression for $a(x)$ reduces to the constant c_1. Since $b(t)$ is never zero, the product of a and b is zero at $x = 0$ only if this constant vanishes. At the other endpoint, the product of a and b must also be zero, but if we let $c_2 = 0$, then $u(x,t)$ is identically zero for all x and t, which is untenable. Therefore, $\sin(d^{1/2}L)$ must be zero at $x = L$. The smallest value of L for which this is true is $L = \pi/d^{1/2}$, which shows that $d = (\pi/L)^2$. Finally, we see that if $r - Dd$ is negative, then $u(x,t)$ tends to zero as t goes to infinity, as is evident from Eq.(5.11); but we are seeking conditions that guarantee a sustainable growth within the patch and so we insist that $r - Dd$ be nonnegative. Using the value of d obtained earlier, this gives the condition $r - D(\pi/L)^2 \geq 0$, or, put another way,

$$L \geq \pi\left(\frac{D}{r}\right)^{1/2}. \tag{5.13}$$

The right side of this inequality is the critical patch size, the smallest width that allows the algae to provide a sufficient number of new recruits to replace those lost by dispersion. Anything smaller and the reproductive ability of the organisms is outstripped by diffusion. Note that as the percapita growth rate r increases, the critical size is allowed to get smaller, whereas if dispersion increases, as measured by the constant D, L must also increase. Both results are consonant with what we expect.

It has been observed that actual bloom patches appear to vary in size from about 10 to 100 kilometers in the open sea and from about one to 10 kilometers in more protected coastal embayments. Allowing the growth rate r to vary from .10 to one cell division per day, a figure that is about right in temperate zone waters, and using estimates of the diffusion coefficient D that are worked out in the book by Okubo listed in Section 5.8, the critical radius obtained from the model gives values of between 2 and 50 kilometers, which is in reasonable accord with observations.

Before closing this section, let us remark on a simplifying assumption that may be both pertinent and useful. If the plankton patch persists for some time, until it eventually disintegrates under the action of wind and tide, then the processes of growth and dispersion reach a sort of equilibrium in which the accumulation of algae appear to reach a stable configuration in space that changes not at all, or at least very little, over time. Under this circumstance, one can approximate the function $u(x,t)$ by a function $u(x)$ of space alone. This is known as a *steady-state assumption*, and since u_t is now zero, it permits us to rewrite Eq.(5.9) as an ordinary differential equation:

$$u''(x) + (r/D)u(x) = 0. \tag{5.14}$$

This equation has an explicit solution (see Appendix B) that is proportional to $\sin((r/D)^{1/2}x)$, if one employs the conditions $u(0) = u(L) = 0$. Thus, u attains a maximum at $x = L/2 = (D/r)^{1/2}\pi/2$.

5.4. Red Tide II

For the sake of completeness, we want to indicate how the argument goes when we allow the patch to be a two-dimensional region of the plane. Since the discussion makes a bit more use of the multivariate calculus, some readers may prefer to regard this section as optional reading, especially since, as we have already remarked, the conclusions reached do not differ significantly from those obtained previously.

We begin by showing what Eq.(5.7) looks like in the context of two spatial dimensions x and y, since this is more appropriate to algal motion that takes place on the surface of the sea or, as will be seen later, to the terrestrial migrations of squirrels along grasslands and woods.

The arguments are really a repetition of what was done before, except that motion takes place in a plane instead of along a line, with the continuous distribution $u(x, t)$ replaced by $u(x, y, t)$.

Consider a region R in the plane enclosed by a smooth curve C, whose coordinates are parametrized by $\mathbf{r}(s) = (x(s), y(s))$, where s denotes arc length. The tangent to the curve at s is therefore given by the derivative $\mathbf{r}'(s) = (x'(s), y'(s))$. Employing the notation $\mathbf{a}^T\mathbf{b}$ for the inner product of two vectors $\mathbf{a}$ and $\mathbf{b}$, we see that the row vector $\mathbf{r}'$ is orthogonal to the transpose of the row vector $\mathbf{n}$ defined by $\mathbf{n}(s) = (y(s), -x(s))$, for all s, and we say that $\mathbf{n}$ is normal to the curve C (see Appendix C). The vector $\mathbf{n}$ is perpendicular to C and points out of R.

The total mass of the particles inside R is given by the double integral of the concentration u over R, and its time rate of change is, as before, the derivative with respect to t, taken inside the integral sign:

$$\int\int_R u_t(x, y, t)dx\, dy. \tag{5.15}$$

The conservation of mass argument stipulates that the rate of change in mass of particles in R, as given by Eq.(5.15) must equal the net flow of particles across the boundary of R plus any additional sources and sinks within R. As before, the rate of flow of sources and sinks is some known function $w(x, y, t)$ measured as concentration per unit time.

Let $\mathbf{q}(x, y, t)$ be the flow of particles in units of mass per unit time. This is a column vector with components $q_i, i = 1, 2$. Since $\mathbf{n}$ is an outward normal to C, the inner product $\mathbf{q}^T\mathbf{n}$ is the component of $\mathbf{q}$ in the outward direction, and the integral of this quantity over C is the net outward flow of particles from R:

$$-\int_C \mathbf{q}^T \mathbf{n} ds. \tag{5.16}$$

The minus sign indicates that an outflow decreases the mass within R. Now we invoke the same Fick's law that was used in the one-dimensional case by stipulating that the two components q_1 and q_2 of the row vector $\mathbf{q}$ are proportional to the derivatives of $\mathbf{u}$ in the x and y directions: $q_1 = -cu_x$ and $q_2 = -cu_y$. In vector notation, this is $\mathbf{q} = -c\nabla \mathbf{u}$, where $\nabla \mathbf{u}$ denotes the gradient vector of $\mathbf{u}$ with components u_x and u_y.

The line integral (5.16) can now be written as

$$-\int_C \mathbf{q}^T \mathbf{n}\, ds = -\int_C (q_1 y' - q_2 x')\, ds = -c\int_C (u_y x' - u_x y')\, ds, \tag{5.17}$$

and, by Green's theorem in the calculus, the line integral on the right of Eq.(5.17) equals the double integral

$$c\int\int_R (u_{xx} + u_{yy})\, dx\, dy. \tag{5.18}$$

Combining Eq.(5.18) with Eq.(5.15) and remembering the source function w, conservation of mass tells us that

$$\int\int_R (u_t - c\nabla^2 \mathbf{u} - w)\, dx\, dy = 0,$$

where $\nabla^2 \mathbf{u} = u_{xx} + u_{yy}$. Since R was chosen to be any set in the plane that is bounded by a smooth curve, the integrand is itself zero for all x and y. Otherwise, if we suppose that the integrand is positive, for example, at some point in the plane, one can find a small disc I about that point in which the integrand remains positive. This is true by virtue of the fact that $u_t - c\nabla^2 u - w$ is a continuous function and so cannot change its sign abruptly. It follows that the double integral of this quantity over I is also positive, which is a contradiction. The two-dimensional diffusion equation is therefore

$$u_t - D\nabla^2 \mathbf{u} - w = 0, \tag{5.19}$$

in which we write c as D to remind us of the diffusion coefficient.

In problems with circular symmetry, such as a two-dimensional flow of particles that is *isotropic* (meaning that the flow depends on radial distance but not on the angle chosen), Eq.(5.19) can be written differently. Make a change of variables by letting $x = r \cdot \cos\Theta$ and $y = r \cdot \sin\Theta$ and define a function v by $v(r,t) = u(r \cdot \cos\Theta, r \cdot \sin\Theta, t)$, independent of Θ. Using the chain rule of differentiation for two variables, one can show (Exercise 5.7.2) that

$$u_{xx} + u_{yy} = \frac{v_r}{r} + v_{rr},$$

and therefore, with $W(r,t) = w(x,y,t)$, the diffusion equation becomes

$$v_t = \frac{Dv_r}{r} + Dv_{rr} + W. \tag{5.20}$$

After this lengthy digression, let us return to the *red tide* and assume a circular region in which the concentration varies with the radial distance r from the center of the patch but not with direction. This isotropy condition reflects the belief that, in the turbulent diffusion of the ocean, we have little reason to bias the flow along any particular path. To avoid confusion, write the percapita growth rate as s instead of r, reserving r for radius. Then we adopt the diffusion equation (5.20), in which $W(r,t) = sv(r,t)$:

$$v_t = \frac{Dv_r}{r} + Dv_{rr} + sv. \tag{5.21}$$

The function $v(r,t)$ equals $u(x,y,t)$ in polar coordinates. We wish to find the minimum radius L that can sustain a bloom. Outside of a circle of this radius, the conditions for growth are unfavorable, and so we impose the requirement that $v(L,t) = 0$.

Using the device of separating variables that we employed earlier, let $v(r,t) = a(r)b(t)$. Then, in an identical manner, one obtains two ordinary differential equations

$$\begin{aligned} b_t - (s - Dd)b &= 0, \\ ra_{rr} + a_r + dsa &= 0. \end{aligned} \tag{5.22}$$

The first of these equations is the same as the first equation in (5.10) except that $c = -d$. The second equation, however, may be less familiar and is called *Bessel's equation*, after the German astronomer

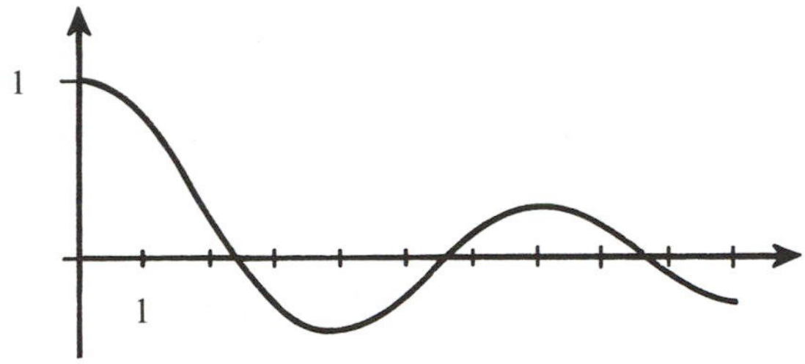

Figure 5.1. Sketch of the Bessel function $J_0(x)$.

F.W. Bessel. Rather than dwell on the details, we simply point out that this equation possesses a solution, the *Bessel function of the first kind of order zero*, that remains finite when $r = 0$. There is also another solution, the *Bessel function of the second kind*, that becomes unbounded as r approaches zero and that is discarded, since this gives a physically unacceptable solution. The Bessel function we use is denoted by $J_0(d^{1/2}r)$ and has a behavior that is not unlike that of $\cos(d^{1/2}r)$ in that it has the value one when $r = 0$ and then oscillates, with its first zero at $d^{1/2}r = 2.405$, whereas the first zero of $\cos(d^{1/2}r)$ is at $\pi/2$ (Fig. 5.1). Sections 13.1 and 13.2 of the book by Redheffer, referred to in Section 4.2, supply the missing details on solving the Bessel equation.

Proceeding now exactly as in the one-dimensional case, we obtain a similar lower bound on L, namely,

$$L \geq 2.405(D/s)^{1/2},$$

which differs slightly from our previous estimate of the critical L only in that the constant π is replaced by 2.405.

5.5. Pollution Susceptibility

Pollutants that are discharged into restricted embayments as sewage effluents or as runoff are partially cleansed by the flushing action of the tides. The open sea is often regarded as an unlimited sink for contaminants, a simplifying assumption that allows us to focus on

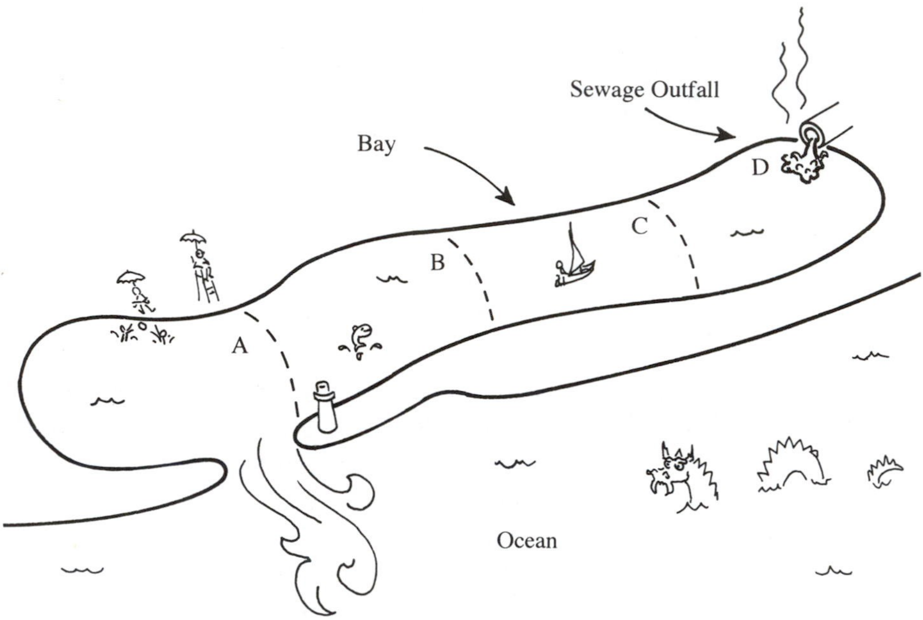

Figure 5.2. A hypothetical bay with a pollution source.

the concentration of pollutants within a body of water of limited size that is nearly hemmed in by coastline. What we have in mind is a bay that has a restricted outlet to the ocean at one end, such as the one illustrated in Fig. 5.2.

To assess the impact of wastes discharged into various parts of the bay, we need to quantify the long-term pollutant concentration that results from the interplay of tidal cleansing, on the one hand, and the continual loading of the bay with pollutants from the adjacent land, on the other. Environmental consultants often utilize sophisticated models that detail the hydrodynamics of estuaries and bays, but for our purposes a simpler approach will provide useful, if perhaps less accurate, assessments.

Let us assume then that the pollutants discharged into the bay at the location D shown in the figure are totally miscible with the water. We will be interested in long-term conditions in the bay, long after discharges have begun, when the pollutant concentrations have reached equilibrium with respect to tidal movement. The approach used is tantamount to a steady-state model, in contrast to more elaborate versions that follow short-term, highly variable disturbances, such as those caused by a storm event in which there is a surge of pollutants into the bay as runoff.

Take, as a surrogate for the pollutant, a dye that is injected into the bay. When the dye is dumped, two things happen. First, because of the movement of the water itself in each tidal cycle, some of the dye is carried seaward and is eventually lost in what is an infinite ocean sink, never to return. Second, over several successive cycles, the pollutant plume folds back and forth as a result of advective flow in one direction during an ebb tide, and then in the reverse direction during a flood tide. Additional dispersion takes place because of diffusion (consider what happens when a dye is put into a full but perfectly still bathtub), but this is disregarded here. Eventually, the dye has spread throughout the bay and its concentration settles down to a value that varies only with location. This is the steady-state condition referred to earlier. Of course, we assume that the dye is being continuously discharged at the outfall site, for otherwise, with no additional infusion, the concentration in the bay would ultimately be completely dissipated. Thus, steady state reflects a net balance between the amount injected into the bay and the dye lost to the ocean in each cycle after complete mixing has taken place.

Define the tidal excursion as the average distance traveled by the dye in each tidal cycle. In Fig. 5.2, we see dotted contour lines, each of which represents a tidal excursion moving landward from the inlet at A. For instance, a dye injected at B would move to A during an ebb tide and as far as C during the ensuing flood tide.

Let $u(x, t)$ be the steady-state pollutant concentration and $q(x, t)$ the flow rate in the bay as measured along the one-dimensional longitudinal direction from A to D in Fig. 5.2, assuming, for simplicity, that u does not vary significantly in the vertical direction. In effect, this says that the concentration changes only with distance to the ocean inlet, a tenable approximation. In each ebb tide, the water flows from right to left for six hours, roughly, and then reverses itself during the flood tide of equal duration. Thus, a tidal cycle consists of two advective motions in opposite directions. This suggests that u satisfies the advective equation (5.8) during each half of the tidal cycle. Recall that the advective equation is given by

$$u_t = -(vu)_x + w, \tag{5.23}$$

which we now approximate to obtain a simple rule of thumb for pollution susceptibility. First, partition the bay into segments consisting of blocks of water extending from the boundary of one tidal excursion to the next. From Fig. 5.2, we obtain three segments, but in general there could be many more, in the vertical as well the horizontal direction, depending on the actual bay/ocean configuration. However, the computational scheme to be discussed presently would be carried out in a similar manner in all cases.

We assume that the pollutant is uniformly mixed in each segment and that the concentration u (mass/volume) is constant within each of these. All changes in u take place between segments and not within them. Moreover, the velocity v of the flow (volume/time) is directed into and out of a segment at its boundaries, and so the only values of v that we need are at the points A, B, or C, denoted as v_1, v_2 and v_3, respectively. The approximation is carried out by considering separately the three segments, each of which has a longitudinal length Δx, representing a single tidal excursion of duration Δt during either an ebb tide or a flood tide. Let u_i be the pollution concentration in segments $i = 1, 2, 3$ and Δu_i the change in u_i during each half of a tidal cycle. Then u_t is approximated by $\Delta u_i / \Delta t$ in segment i, while $(vu)_x$ can be written as the difference in vu between the two boundaries of segment i, divided by the volume V_i of the segment. Equation (5.23) now represents the value of u during an ebb tide, segment by segment, as:

$$\begin{aligned} \frac{V_1 \Delta u_1}{\Delta t} &= -(v_1 u_1 - v_2 u_2), \\ \frac{V_2 \Delta u_2}{\Delta t} &= -(v_2 u_2 - v_3 u_3), \\ \frac{V_3 \Delta u_3}{\Delta t} &= -(v_3 u_3 - W), \end{aligned} \tag{5.24}$$

where W is the effluent discharge rate (mass/time). Note that w in Eq.(5.23) is obtained from W by dividing it by the volume of the water.

Similarly, during a flood tide, one gets

$$\begin{aligned}
\frac{V_1 \Delta u_1}{\Delta t} &= -v_2 u_1, \\
\frac{V_2 \Delta u_2}{\Delta t} &= v_2 u_1 - v_3 u_2, \\
\frac{V_3 \Delta u_3}{\Delta t} &= v_3 u_2 + W.
\end{aligned} \tag{5.25}$$

Observe that in the first equation of (5.25), there is no pollutant flow into segment 1, since the ocean returns only clean water at each flood tide. This is also reflected in the first equation of (5.24) in which $v_1 u_1$ is the loss of pollutant into the open sea, never to return.

In a steady-state mode, we expect Δu_i over a flood tide to be equal in value but opposite in sign to Δu_i over an ebb tide, for each i. Employing this fact gives us the following set of equations, utilizing Eqs.(5.24) and (5.25):

$$\begin{aligned}
v_2 u_2 - v_1 u_1 &= v_2 u_1, \\
v_2 u_2 - v_3 u_3 &= v_2 u_1 - v_3 u_2, \\
v_3 u_3 - W &= v_3 u_2 + W.
\end{aligned}$$

These algebraic relations can be readily solved and we find that

$$\begin{aligned}
u_1 &= \frac{2W}{v_1}, \\
u_2 &= \frac{2W}{v_2} + u_1, \\
u_3 &= \frac{2W}{v_3} + u_2.
\end{aligned} \tag{5.26}$$

This shows, not surprisingly, that the pollution concentration increases as one moves inward along the bay, away from the ocean inlet. A similar result would be found if the pollutant discharge were located at some other point (Exercise 5.7.6).

Consider a 1 km^3 block of water that moves with the tide. If, in the steady state, a ton of pollutant is fully mixed into that volume, then, since 1 km^3 of water weighs about 10^9 tons, it follows that the pollutant concentration is 10^{-9} (one part per billion, or ppb for short) in each such block. Depending on the total volume of water that is flushed out to sea (km^3/time) and on the effluent discharge rate W (tons/time), the concentrations will of course vary. Bays with poor tidal circulation can be expected to have higher than normal pollutant concentrations.

Assuming a continuous discharge of one ton per Δt, the steady state *pollution susceptibility* in each segment of the bay is defined as the long-term concentration in ppb that occurs there. If the bay is fed by a significant river discharge, as would be the case in an estuary, then the resulting concentration would be less, since the total flow towards the ocean is now greater. Also, if the pollutant is not conservative, in the sense that it decays in the water over time due to bacterial action, then the long-term concentrations as given here would be somewhat inflated. Therefore, the present model is likely to be an overestimate of the actual pollution susceptibility.

Since W is assumed known and the v_i can be calculated from hydrographic data, the pollution concentration may be found from Eq.(5.26), and susceptibility is then the special case of $W = 1$ ton per Δt. This simple scheme yields a remarkably good indicator of how vulnerable the embayment is to actual pollution loadings.

For another use of the advective equation (5.23), consider a river that moves downstream along the positive x axis at a constant velocity v. There is a constant pollutant discharge of W tons/time at position $x = 0$, which we choose to regard as a boundary condition for the equation instead of incorporating it as a separate source term. Therefore $u_t = -vu_x$, with $u(0,t) = W$.

Now suppose that the pollutant is some organic detritus that decays in the water as a result of bacterial action at a rate that is proportional to the concentration u of the pollutant. This is a loss term in the advective equation, in which $w = -ku$, for some constant of proportionality k that is measured in units of 1/time. Thus,

$$u_t = -vu_x - ku. \tag{5.27}$$

As the pollutant decomposes, it depletes the supply of oxygen dissolved in the river, since the bacteria utilize oxygen to metabolize the debris. The loss of oxygen occurs at the same rate that substance of density u is decaying. However, there is also a supply of oxygen due to the effect of re-oxygenation (self purification) of the river through surface to air contact. If $p(x,t)$ is the concentration of dissolved oxygen at time t and position x and if $p_{\max}$ is the saturation value of oxygen in water(an empirically determined constant), then the re-oxygenation term is proportional to the amount of oxygen deficit $p_{\max} - p$ at any time. The constant of proportionality k_1 also has units of 1/time, and we assume that $k_1 > k$. The advective equation for p is accordingly

$$p_t = -vp_x - ku + k_1(p_{\max} - p). \tag{5.28}$$

We now seek a steady state, or time-independent solution, to the pair of equations (5.27) and (5.28), in the spirit of our discussion at the end of Section 5.3. We know that $u(0) = W$ and one is also given an initial value for $p(0)$. The equations are now ordinary differential equations in the variable x and are given by

$$u'(x) + \frac{k}{v}u(x) = 0,$$
$$p'(x) + \frac{k}{v}u(x) - \frac{k_1}{v}(p_{\max} - p(x)) = 0. \tag{5.29}$$

The first of these equations is readily solvable. Substituting this into the second of the equations gives a single equation in p that is linear but nonhomogeneous (see Section 6.1 of the book by Redheffer referenced in Section 4.7 for details), and so has an explicit solution that shows how the oxygen deficit varies with distance from the pollutant source along the river (Exercise 5.7.7). Since the amount of dissolved oxygen is considered a measure of the health of a body of water, this computation is of some interest to environmental engineers.

5.6. The Spread of the Gray Squirrel

When the American gray squirrel was released into the English countryside about the turn of the century, it was faced with a competitor, the indigenous red squirrel, that occupied the same habitats and had similar food preferences and foraging habits. Some red squirrels fell prey to a disease, possibly transmitted from its gray cousin, but, perhaps more significantly, it was outcompeted by the more prolific

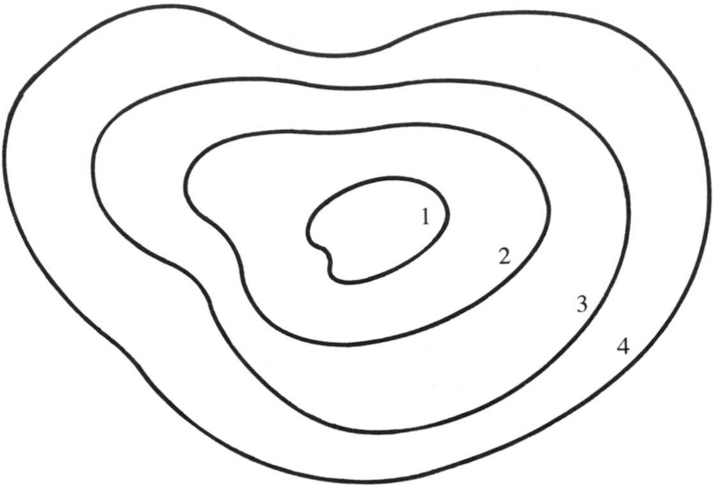

Figure 5.3. Sketch of a typical dispersion in space, with contours marking the propagation over four successive years.

breeding and larger size of the American. As time went on, the intruder began to colonize new areas, mostly woodlands, as the original sites became overcrowded. As the invading grays advanced forward, they largely replaced the reds that had already settled there. The two species coexisted for a time as the concentration of the grays increased and that of the reds diminished. To all appearances then, the changes in population densities were waves moving outward in space as time evolved, two waves out of phase as the gray squirrel progressively colonized new areas and the red squirrel receded (Fig. 5.3).

The idea now is to model the wave-like behavior of the invading squirrels by using the diffusion equation (5.6) to represent the spatial spread of these mammals along a single axis of motion. In addition, the interaction between the two species is modeled in terms of the competition equations derived in Section 4.2. These play the role of w, the net source terms, in the diffusion equation. The restriction to a one-dimensional movement is done for reasons of mathematical expediency but does not seriously detract from the interpretative value of the model.

Let $u(x,t)$ and $v(x,t)$ be the population densities of the gray and red squirrels, respectively, which are assumed, as usual, to be twice continuously differentiable functions in x and t. Then, combining Eq.(5.7) with Eq.(4.5), we obtain a pair of equations:

$$\begin{aligned} u_t &= D_1 u_{xx} + ru\left(1 - \frac{u}{K}\right) - auv, \\ v_t &= D_2 v_{xx} + sv\left(1 - \frac{v}{L}\right) - buv, \end{aligned} \tag{5.30}$$

in which the competition terms represent sources and sinks. In a paper referred to in the next section, the net percapita birth rates r and s are estimated to be .82 and .61 per year, respectively, with maximum population densities of 10 and .75 per hectare (which is 10^4 square meters). The diffusion coefficients are taken to be the same, at about 18 kilometers squared per year. The competition coefficients a and b are difficult to estimate from the available data, but it was reasonable to assume that a is less than b, since the grays outcompete the reds and it was decided to pick $a = .5, b = 1.5$.

In the interest of seeing what is at least theoretically possible, the model is simplified even more by scaling all the variables so that many of the coefficients reduce to unity. This will permit us to obtain at least some insight into the model structure by analytical means. Later, the results of a numerical simulation of the full model are compared to actual field observations. The drastically simplified equations are then

$$\begin{aligned} u_t &= u_{xx} + u(1-u) - auv, \\ v_t &= v_{xx} + v(1-v) - buv, \end{aligned} \tag{5.31}$$

with $a < 1, b > 1$, and $a + b = 2$.

In the absence of diffusion and spatial dependence (so that, in particular, $u_{xx} = v_{xx} = 0$), the system (5.31) consists of coupled ordinary differential equations with equilibria at

$$\begin{pmatrix} u \\ v \end{pmatrix} = \begin{pmatrix} 0 \\ 0 \end{pmatrix}, \begin{pmatrix} 0 \\ 1 \end{pmatrix}, \begin{pmatrix} 1 \\ 0 \end{pmatrix}$$

in the nonnegative quadrant of the u, v plane. A nullcline analysis shows that the first two points are unstable, but that the last

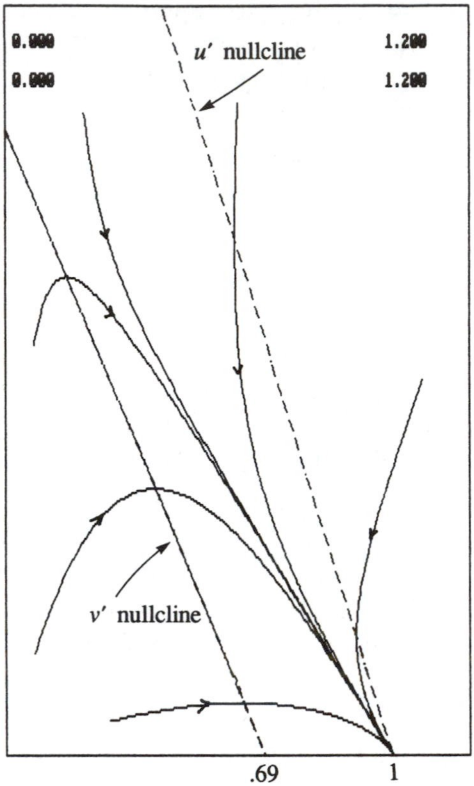

Figure 5.4. Nullclines for the equations $u' = u(1-u) - auv, v' = v(1-v) - buv$ when $a < 1, b > 1$, with typical trajectories.

equilibrium is an attractor (Fig. 5.4 and Exercise 5.7.3; see also the discussion of equilibria and nullclines in Section 4.2).

Fig. 5.4 demonstrates that it is possible for trajectories to flow towards the point $u = 1, v = 0$, in which the gray squirrels have outcompeted the reds. It is another version of the paradigm that when two species are in strongly overlapping niches, one of them is inexorably driven to extinction.

We now return to the partial differential equations (5.31) and look for wave-like solutions. These *travelling wave* solutions are of the form $u(x,t) = f(s)$ and $v(x,t) = h(s)$, where $s = x - qt$ for $q > 0$. The functions f and h are monotone in s and move parallel to them-

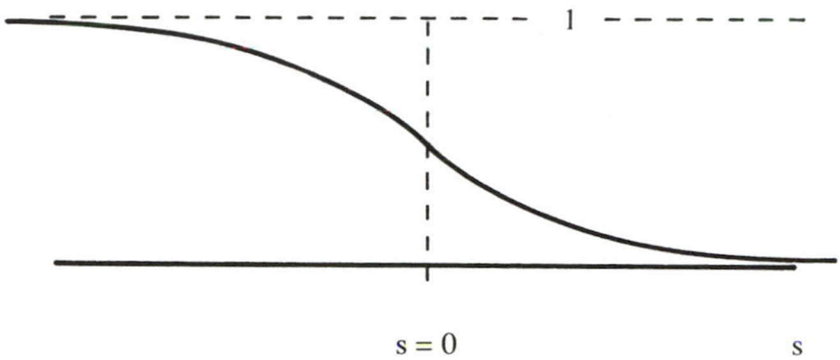

Figure 5.5. A wave-like function $f(s)$.

selves in the positive x direction with constant shape as t increases. To see how this comes about, suppose that f, for example, has the form exhibited in Fig. 5.5, which is asymptotic to 1 at $s = -\infty$ and is asymptotic to 0 at $t = +\infty$. Then, for any fixed position x, $s = x - qt$ goes to $-\infty$ as $t \to +\infty$, and a little reflection shows that $f(s)$ moves to the right at a constant speed q while maintaining its shape (Fig. 5.6). In effect, $f(s)$ increases, for a given position x and speed q, only if $s = x - qt$ moves to the left, and that occurs only as t increases. These are the travelling waves we seek.

Substituting the functions f and h into Eqs(5.31) produces a pair of ordinary differential equations in the single variable s, in which all derivatives are indicated by a prime, as in Chapter 4:

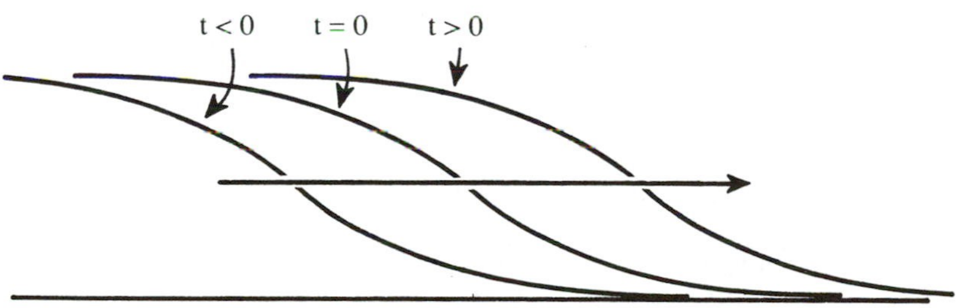

Figure 5.6. The function $f(s) = f(x - qt)$ for x and q fixed, as $t \to +\infty$. This gives rise to traveling waves.

$$
\begin{aligned}
-qf' &= f'' + f(1-f) - afh, \\
-qh' &= h'' + h(1-h) - bfh.
\end{aligned}
\tag{5.32}
$$

Since $a+b=2$, this set of equations can be added together to obtain a single equation in the variable $z(s) = f(s)+h(s)$, which, as is easily verified, satisfies

$$
-qz' = z'' + z(1-z). \tag{5.33}
$$

This is known as *Fisher's equation*, after the English statistician R.A. Fisher.

We look for traveling wave solutions to Eqs.(5.32) in order to mimic the spatial spread of gray squirrels as they overtake the reds. In the remote past, the reds are at high concentrations and the grays are low, but as time elapses their status at any given location is reversed. To reflect this, we impose the conditions that $f(s) = 0, h(s) = 1$ at $s = \infty$, while $f(s) = 1, h(s) = 0$ at $s = -\infty$. This means that for any fixed x, the red squirrels are dominant as t moves towards negative infinity (the distant past), with just the opposite as t advances to the distant future. In terms of the sum $z(s)$, this translates into $z(s) = 1$ at $\pm\infty$. We will show next that this implies that $z(s)$ is identically equal to unity for all s. It follows that $f(s) = 1 - h(s)$. Substituting this into the first of Eqs.(5.32), one gets

$$
-qf' = f'' + f(1-f-ah) = (1-a)f(1-f) + f'', \tag{5.34}
$$

which is another form of Fisher's equation, this time with the conditions $f(-\infty) = 1, f(+\infty) = 0$.

The second-order equation (5.34) may be rewritten as a pair of first-order equations in a new set of variables x_1 and x_2 by letting $x_1 = f$ and $x_2 = f'$. This gives us

$$
\begin{aligned}
x_1' &= x_2, \\
x_2' &= -qx_2 - (1-a)x_1(1-x_1),
\end{aligned}
\tag{5.35}
$$

where a is of course less than one.

The only equilibria of Eqs.(5.35) are at

$$
\begin{pmatrix} x_1 \\ x_2 \end{pmatrix} = \begin{pmatrix} 0 \\ 0 \end{pmatrix} \quad \text{and} \quad \begin{pmatrix} 1 \\ 0 \end{pmatrix},
$$

and by looking at the signs of the derivatives we can reveal something of the structure of the solutions, much as was done in the preceding chapter. For example, it is always true that $x_1' = x_2 > 0$ in the positive quadrant of the x_1, x_2 plane, whereas it is always negative in the lower right-hand quadrant, where $x_2 < 0$. This already tells us that trajectories move to the right (left) in the upper (lower) half planes separated by the horizontal axis, where $x_2 = 0$. Since $x_1' = 0$ on this axis (the $x_1' = 0$ nullcline), the axis is necessarily crossed in a vertical direction. Therefore, a trajectory that emanates from the equilibrium state $x_1 = 1, x_2 = 0$ can never return there, since it would have to move to the left in the lower plane and return to the right along the upper plane; but the derivative x_2' is always negative in the positive quadrant whenever $x < 1$, and so not only do the trajectories move to the right there, but they also slope downward. This precludes a closed trajectory that begins and ends at the equilibrium state other than the equilibrium state itself, of course, which is a constant solution to Eqs.(5.35).

We should be clear here that any solution that emanates from or tends toward an equilibrium solution can never actually reach this state, since this would mean that two distinct solutions begin at the same point in the plane, which is a violation of the uniqueness principle for differential equations.(See Section 4.2.) Therefore, although it is possible for a trajectory to approach the equilibrium $x_1 = 1$, $x_2 = 0$ arbitrarily close as s tends to infinity, or, reversing the direction of the flow, as s tends to negative infinity, it cannot loop back to this point. If you think of s as *time*, this idea is easier to grasp.

After this digression, we return to Eq.(5.33) which, after all, is a special case of Eq.(5.34), in which $a = 0$, and confirm that indeed $z(s)$ must be constant in s, since it represents a solution that begins and ends at the equilibrium where $z = x_1 = 1, z' = x_2 = 0$.

As for Eqs.(5.35), the argument just given supports the possibility of a solution that emanates from the unstable equilibrium at $x_1 = 1$, $x_2 = 0$ and moves to the stable point at the origin. A formal argument can be given to verify that this is in fact true, and a numerical solution of Eqs.(5.35) exhibits what appears to be just such a trajectory (Fig. 5.7). This provides a traveling wave solution to the first equation of (5.32), with the desired properties that $f = x_1 = 1$ at $s = -\infty$ and $f = 0$ at $s = +\infty$. Moreover, since the solution

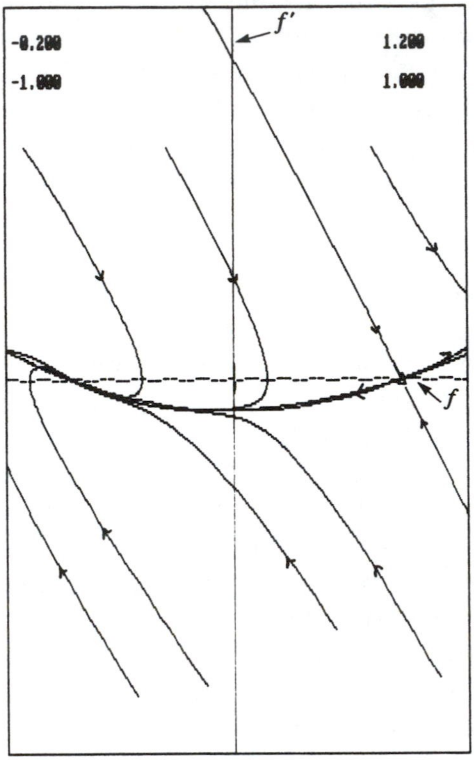

Figure 5.7. Trajectories of the Equation (5.34), in which we see a single trajectory that links two equilibria from $f = 1$ to $f = 0$, where f' is zero. This corresponds to a traveling wave solution to the first equation in Eq.(5.32).

lies in the lower half plane , it means that $f' = x_2$ is negative and, therefore, that f is monotone decreasing, as required.

We close our discussion by estimating the minimum wave speed q and then comparing it to the empirically observed spread of the gray squirrel.

Imagine that a line L passes through the origin of the x_1, x_2 plane with negative slope $-lx_2, l > 0$. If we can show that all trajectories cross this line inwardly (in an upward direction), then any solution that moves from $f = 1$ to $f = 0$ in the f, f' plane (namely, the x_1, x_2 plane) would never be able reach the origin through negative values of f, since it would be confined to the triangular region made up of the horizontal line $x_2 = 0$, the vertical axis defined by $x_1 = 1$, and the line L. Such a triangle is displayed by dotted lines in Fig. 5.7. All trajectories cross into the triangle, and so, in particular, the one emanating from $f = 1, f' = 0$ never gets to be negative. This is important since a negative f implies a negative population density, which is biologically unfeasible. The existence of L is linked to the value of q, as will now be seen.

The line L has coordinates $(x_1, x_2) = x_1(1, -l)$ and the normal to L is the column vector $\mathbf{n}$ that we write in row form as $(l, 1)$. The inner product between $\mathbf{n}$ and $(1, -l)$ is zero, and so $\mathbf{n}$ is perpendicular to L and points up and to the right of the line. The solution to Eqs.(5.35) is the vector $\mathbf{x}(s)$ with components $x_i(s)$, and the derivative $x'(s)$ has components $x_i'(s)$; x' is tangent to the trajectory and points in the direction of the flow. Recalling that the inner product of two vectors is a measure of the cosine of the angle between them, it follows that any trajectory that crosses L does so in an inward direction, whenever the inner product between $\mathbf{n}$ and $\mathbf{x}'$ is positive, since they differ in direction by an angle that is less than $\pi/2$. What needs to be demonstrated then is that the inner product between $(l, 1)$ and the column vector with components $x_2, -qx_2 - (1-a)x_1(1-x_1)$ is positive along L. Using the fact that $x_2 = -lx_1$ along L, it means that $-l^2x_1 + qlx_1 - (1-a)x_1(1-x_1)$ is positive or, factoring out x_1, the requirement is that

$$l^2 - ql + (1-a)(1-x_1) \leq l^2 - ql + (1-a) < 0,$$

since this gives the positivity we are after (note: $0 \leq x_1 \leq 1$).

The quadratic $l^2 - ql + (1-a)$ is positive when l is zero and when l is sufficiently large. Therefore, the quadratic can be negative only if it has two positive roots; but the roots of $l^2 - ql + (1-a)$ are readily computed to be $l = q/2 \pm \left(q^2 - 4(1-a)\right)^{1/2}/2$ and so are real and positive only if $q^2 \geq 4(1-a)$. It follows that there is a critical minimum speed q defined by

$$q \geq 2(1-a)^{1/2} \tag{5.36}$$

if there is to be a feasible traveling wave solution.

Observe that if $h(s) = z(s) - f(s)$ is now inserted into the second equation of (5.34), another form of Fisher's equation is obtained, this time for the function h:

$$-qh' = h'' - (b-1)h(1-h), \tag{5.37}$$

with $b > 1$. The conditions on h are $h(-\infty) = 0$ and $h(+\infty) = 1$. An analysis that is similar to the one just concluded for Eqs.(5.35) also applies to Eq.(5.37) (Exercise 5.7.4), showing that there is a minimum speed q given by $q \geq 2(b-1)^{1/2}$; but $a + b = 2$ and so the minimum speeds for f and h are the same. The gray and red squirrels advance and recede at the same rate.

In a study done by Okubo and others (see the references in Section 5.8), the minimum speed is estimated from observations to be about 7.7 kilometers per year. This is how fast the gray squirrel encroaches on new terrain occupied by the red squirrels. Using estimates of growth rates and diffusion that were mentioned earlier, the model predicts a wave speed of 7.66 kilometers per year.

5.7. Exercises

5.7.1. Consider a random walk on the integers $0, 1, \dots N$ with one-step transition probabilities $p_{i,i+1} = p, p_{i,i-1} = q, p+q = 1, p_{0,0} = p_{N,N} = 1$, and $pi, j = 0$ for all other i, j. In the terminology of Chapter 1, this is a Markov chain on $N + 1$ states, in which 0 and N are absorbing states. Let b_i be the probability of ever reaching state N if the process begins in state i. (This is $b_{i,N}$ in the notation of Chapter 1.)

State N can be reached from i by first taking one step to the right or left. Conditioning on these disjoint events gives

$$b_i = pb_{i+1} + qb_{i-1}. \tag{5.38}$$

The reasoning here is similar to that employed in deriving Eq.(5.1) in the text. Now b_i is identical to $(p+q)b_i$, and so Eq.(5.38) can be rewritten as

$$p(b_{i+1} - b_i) = q(b_i - b_{i-1}). \tag{5.39}$$

Using the fact that $b_0 = 0$, together with Eq.(5.39), show that

$$b_i = b_1 \sum_{k=0}^{i-1} \left(\frac{q}{p}\right)^k$$

for $i = i, 2, \ldots N-1$.

Now recall the following identity for the partial sum of a geometric series of a scalar a:

$$\sum_{k=0}^{r} a^k = \frac{1 - a^{r+1}}{1 - a}$$

for any integer $r > 0$. From this, and the fact that $b_N = 1$, show that

$$b_i = \begin{cases} \dfrac{1 - (q/p)^i}{1 - (q/p)^N} & p \neq q, \\ \frac{i}{N} & p = q. \end{cases}$$

Compare this result with Exercise 1.5.4 for the case $N = 4$, which was obtained earlier using a different argument.

5.7.2. We are given a smooth function $u(x, y, t)$. Make a change of variables $x = r \cdot \cos\Theta, y = r \cdot \sin\Theta$. If u is independent of Θ, then $u(x, y, t) = v(r, t)$ for some function v. Using the chain rule of differentiation, and the notation of Section 5.4, establish that $u_{xx} + u_{yy} = v_r/r + v_{rr}$.

5.7.3. Assume that u and v are independent of x in Eqs.(5.31) to obtain a pair of ordinary differential equations in the independent variable t. These have three equilibria in the nonnegative quadrant of the u, v plane. Using the nullcline approach developed in Section 4.2, show that two of these are unstable but that the remaining one is an attractor.

5.7.4. Find the minimum wave speed of the traveling wave solution to Eq.(5.37) using an argument similar to that employed for Eqs.(5.34).

5.7.5. In its simplest form, the epidemic model of Chapter 4 consists of two equations, one for the fraction S of susceptibles and the other for the fraction I of infectives (Eqs.(4.16) and Exercise 4.5.9). A third group, the fraction R of recovered individuals is obtained from the relation $S + I + R = 1$.

This model can be extended by allowing for the spatial spread of a disease. A specific case is the propagation of rabies by infected foxes that wander at random through a population of healthy but susceptible foxes. The uninfected animals have territorial instincts that keep them more or less fixed in space, but the sick animals appear to lose their sense of territoriality and they move about. The disease itself is transmitted through the saliva of rabid foxes.

Equations (4.16) are modified by letting S and I be functions of a one-dimensional space axis x as well as time t, with diffusion confined to the rabies infected foxes:

$$\begin{aligned} S_t &= -bSI, \\ I_t &= bSI - cI + DI_{xx}, \end{aligned} \tag{5.40}$$

where D is the diffusion coefficient that measures the rate of dispersion of the sick animals. The contact rate is b, as before, but c now represents the removal rate of sick foxes by death, instead of a recovery rate, since rabies is invariably fatal to the infected animals.

We seek traveling wave solutions to Eqs.(5.40) in the form $s(x,t) = f(z)$ and $I(x,t) = h(z)$, where $z = x - qt$ and $q > 0$ is the wave speed. We suggest you refer to the discussion in Section 5.6 on traveling waves, noting, however, that s has been replaced by the variable z to avoid confusion with S. In the distant past, the population of susceptibles at any position x has the same constant density $S = 1$ (no infectives have turned up yet and there are no deaths of sick animals). A pulse wave of rabid foxes moves through space and decreases the percentage of healthy foxes to some value $S_m > 0$. The pulse is zero in the remote past and in the distant future. (See Fig. 5.8.)

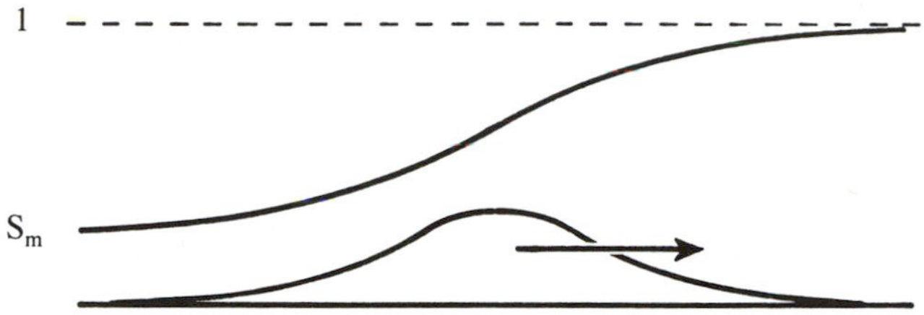

Figure 5.8. A pulse wave of infectives traveling through a territory in which there is a fixed number of susceptibles.

Formulate the proper conditions on f and h at $z = \pm\infty$ to reflect these hypotheses.

Substitute f and h into Eqs.(5.40) and show that

$$\begin{aligned} -qf' &= -bfh, \\ -qh' &= bfh - ch + Dh''. \end{aligned} \tag{5.41}$$

At the leading edge of the moving pulse wave, as the infectives reach the hitherto uninfected foxes, S is close to one in value, so the second equation of (5.41) can be approximated at the leading edge by

$$h'' + qh' + (b - c)h = 0,$$

where D is scaled to one for notational convenience. This is a linear second-order differential equation, and, using standard solution techniques for such equations (see Appendix B), show that the solution h is proportional to the exponential of

$$(-q \pm (q^2 - 4(b-c))^{1/2})\frac{z}{2}.$$

If $q^2 < 4(b-c)$, the solution is complex and $h(z)$ will oscillate about the z axis, taking on positive and negative values alternatively; but we must insist that h remain positive in order that it can represent a biologically feasible population density. Therefore,

$$q \geq 2(b-c)^{1/2}$$

is the minimum wave speed. Note that c/b must be less than one for a positive speed, which is the same threshold condition that was arrived at in Exercise 4.5.9. Even though the reasoning above is based on an approximation, a more careful argument along the lines of that given in Section 5.6 would allow us to reach the same conclusion.

5.7.6. Refer back to Fig. 5.2 and suppose that now the sewage outfall is located at the shoreline near the contour at C. Following the discussion in Section 5.5, establish the analog of the pollution concentration relations found in Eqs.(5.26).

5.7.7 Complete the study of the steady-state equation system (5.29), reducing the pair to a single nonhomogeneous linear equation, as suggested in the text. This gives the dissolved oxygen concentration at any point along the river; you should find that it reaches a minimum at some finite distance downstream from the pollution source, and then it begins to increase again due to the self-purification of the river through re-aeration. The resulting curve showing the oxygen concentration as a function of x is called the *oxygen sag curve* and Eqs.(5.29) are known as the *Streeter-Phelps equations.*

5.8. Further Readings

Recurrent toxic blooms are simply one manifestation of how coastal waters are being stressed by the impact of human activity, and the perception that our waters are deteriorating is cause for increasing anxiety ("Brown Tide hits Peconic and baymen fear worst," *New York Times*, June 30, 1991, and "Algae bloom outbreaks seen in ocean: spread of *red tides* could harm fisheries," *Washington Post*, Oct. 31, 1991).

The plankton patch model follows an early paper on the subject [32], while the squirrel migration model is based on a more recent publication [33]. An overview of diffusion models of algae, insects, and animals is contained in the excellent book by Okubo [34], and we also recommend the substantial treatise by Murray [35] that includes diffusion models in the study of epidemics, as well as a derivation of the diffusion equation.

The idea of pollution susceptibility follows the paper by Weyl [36], although our argument differs considerably in detail.

6

It's All a Game

6.1. Background

In the gripping movie "Run Silent, Run Deep," Clark Gable plays the role of a World War II submarine commander who is obsessed with penetrating enemy defenses without being detected. In one episode, the sub lies motionless in the depths of the ocean, engines shut down, to prevent the enemy from picking up any sounds that would reveal the position of the oblong vessel. The captain of the menacing hulk on the surface is intent on destroying the submarine, and both commanders are engaged in a deadly game of evasion and pursuit.

Another encounter, with economic consequences this time but equally in earnest, is the competition between two individuals or two firms for the right to exploit a common resource. To put this in perspective, we return to the fishery problem of Chapter 4 in which access to a fishery is open to only two participants, each of whom want to maximize their own revenues but are hindered by the presence of the other. This too can be thought of as a game.

The circle of ideas concerning harvesting of resources and competition that were begun earlier in the book are brought together in this chapter and are used to illustrate some elementary techniques in optimization that require the use of calculus.

In the next section, a useful lemma from the calculus of variations is established that is then employed in Section 6.3 to discuss optimal tactics for a submarine and its searcher. The fishery problem is treated next by introducing an optimal strategy between competitors that has a different twist.

6.2. A Variational Lemma

If $f(x)$ is a real valued function of a single variable x, and if f has maximum at some point x_0 in an interval $a < x < b$, then, assuming that f is differentiable in the open interval $a < x < b$, we know from the calculus that $f'(x_0) = 0$, provided that x_0 is not a boundary point. However, if the maximum does occur on the boundary of the interval–at endpoint a, for example–then it is no longer necessarily true that the derivative vanishes there (Fig. 6.1). In fact, $f(a+h) - f(a) < 0$ for all small enough positive h, and so if one divides this difference by h and then takes the one-sided limit $f'_+(a)$ as $h \to 0$ through positive values, the inequality $f'_+(a) \leq 0$ will follow. When f is differentiable at the point a, one can also take the limit as $h \to 0$ along negative values and, in this case, $f'(a) = f'_-(a) = f'_+(a) \leq 0$.

Motivated by this simple calculus argument, consider now a continuously differentiable function f of another function $y(x)$, where y is defined on the interval $a \leq x \leq b$. Suppose that the integral

$$\int_a^b f(x, y(x))\, dx \tag{6.1}$$

attains a maximum for some specific function $y_0(x)$ among all continuously differentiable and nonnegative $y(x)$ having the same values $y(a)$ and $y(b)$. We wish to find a condition on f that must hold at the maximum, similar to the derivative conditions that apply in the simpler scalar case. Just as we considered $f(a+h)$ for nonnegative scalar h earlier, we now write $f(x, y_0(x) + \epsilon h(x))$ for $\epsilon \geq 0$. We say that a continuously differentiable function h is an *admissible variation* if $h(a) = h(b) = 0$ and if the function $y_0 + \epsilon h$ is nonnegative for all x in the interval whenever ϵ is small enough. In particular, we require that h be nonnegative for all x where $y_0(x)$ is zero (Fig. 6.2). The following lemma will be useful in the subsequent section.

Lemma 6.1. *Let y_0 provide a maximum of the integral (6.1) among all continuously differentiable nonnegative functions y having the same values at a and b. Then*

$$\begin{aligned} f_y &= 0 \quad \text{for all } x \text{ where } y_0(x) > 0, \\ f_y &\le 0 \quad \text{for all } x \text{ where } y_0(x) = 0. \end{aligned} \tag{6.2}$$

The subscript y denotes the derivative of f with respect to the argument y.

Proof. Choose an admissible variation h and write

$$F(\epsilon) = \int_a^b f(x, y_0(x) + \epsilon h(x))\, dx.$$

F is real valued and differentiable in ϵ, and it achieves a maximum at $\epsilon = 0$. Taking the derivative of F with respect to ϵ inside the integral sign, our earlier discussion tells us that $F'(0) \le 0$; but

$$F'(\epsilon) = \int_a^b f_y(x, y_0(x) + \epsilon h(x))h(x)\, dx,$$

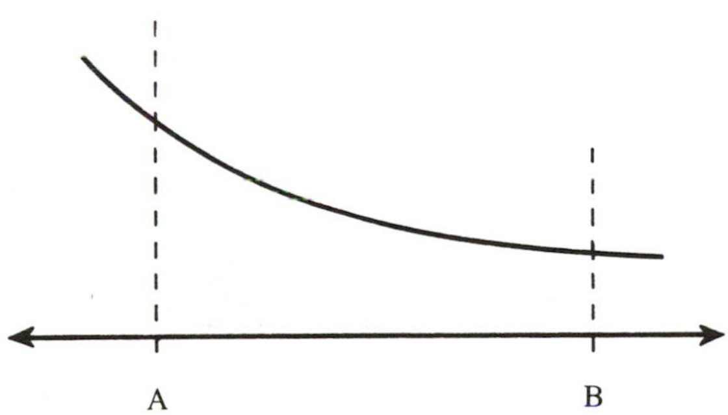

Figure 6.1. The function $f(x)$ has a maximum at $x = a$, where $f' \neq 0$.

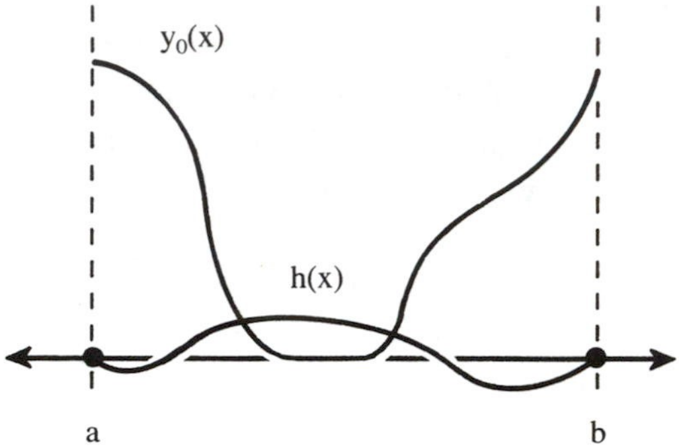

Figure 6.2. An admissible variation $h(x)$.

and so

$$f_y(x, y_0(x))h(x)\,dx \le 0. \tag{6.3}$$

Let $y_0(x)$ be positive at some x in the interval. Then, since y_0 is a smooth function, it continues to be positive in some open interval I about x. Suppose that f_y is positive (negative) at x and choose h to be positive (negative) on I and zero elsewhere (Fig. 6.3). If I is small enough, h is an admissible variation. In either case, Eq.(6.3) becomes an integral over I that is positive. This contradiction shows that f_y must be zero at x. On the other hand, if y_0 is zero at x, then choosing h to be positive on I forces f_y to be non-positive there if we are not to contradict Eq.(6.3). This completes the proof. □

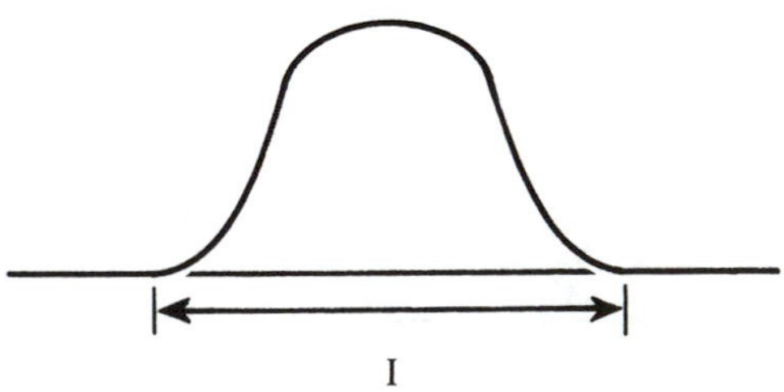

Figure 6.3. A smooth function $h(x)$ that is zero outside I.

6.3. Hide and Seek

A submarine is hiding somewhere within a region R of the ocean while its enemy engages in a search effort by patrolling the surface of R at random either by plane or ship. For ease of presentation, we take R to be an interval of the real x axis.

The erratic movements of the searcher are designed to surprise the sub commander who would otherwise be able to predict the whereabouts of the opposing forces, enabling him to position his vessel so as to minimize detection. The probability of detection, either by visual sighting or by a combination of radar and sonar, depends on the proximity of target and searcher. The amount of effort exerted in searching any given location, in terms of hours spent or miles covered per unit force, has a probability density function $g(x)$ that describes the frequency with which a point x is covered by the random patrol. Given that the target is actually at x, the conditional probability of detection is then $1 - e^{-g(x)}$. This result can be motivated by considering a discrete search consisting of n independent glimpses, each of which has a probability g of detecting the sub. Then the probability that the target escapes detection is, by the assumed independence, $(1 - g)^n$, and so the probability of being observed is one minus this quantity. When n is large, we know from calculus that this expression can be approximated by an exponential: $1-(1 - g)^n \sim 1-e^{-ng}$. Since we are dealing here with a sequence of Bernoulli trials (success or failure of detection), the quantity ng is the average number of successes in n trials. In the case of continuous tracking, in which the glimpses are no longer discrete, ng is replaced by the mean number of sightings per unit time at position x, a quantity that is assumed to be proportional to the effort $g(x)$. Because visibility varies from place to place due to changes in daylight, depth, fog, obstacles, or some other interference, the function g is multiplied by a factor $a(x)$ between zero and one to indicate the efficiency of search at position x. The conditional probability of detection then becomes $1 - e^{a(x)g(x)}$, and therefore, the unconditional probability of finding the hidden sub in the region R is

$$P = \int_R p(x)(1 - e^{-a(x)g(x)})\, dx, \tag{6.4}$$

where $p(x)$ is the probability density function of the target being at x. The choice of p is up to the submarine commander who picks this distribution so as to minimize the quantity P. The integrand in Eq.(6.4) expresses a *law of diminishing returns* in which a doubling of effort results in something less than a doubling of P, even when $a(x)$ is identically one.

The enemy searchers, on the other hand, want to maximize P provided that the cost of doing so is not exorbitant. Let $b(x)$ reflect the cost per unit effort of searching at x in terms of the difficulty or risk incurred. Then the total cost over R is

$$C = \int_R b(x)g(x)\,dx, \tag{6.5}$$

and the searcher wants to maximize Eq.(6.1) while minimizing some multiple r of Eq.(6.5). A large r signifies a relatively high concern for cost, whereas a low value of r means that cost is relatively insignificant in terms of being able to find the target. Now the minimum of C is the same as the maximum of $-C$, as a little reflection will reveal, and so the searcher's goal is to maximize a weighted sum $P - rC$.

The searcher must choose g while the opponent has the option of selecting p, and both do so optimally. What we wish to show next is how the two opposing players decide on their strategies.

We begin by maximizing $P - rC$ by choosing a smooth function g. Clearly, g must be nonnegative and so Lemma 6.1 is applicable in which the function f is now

$$p(x)(1 - e^{-a(x)g(x)}) - rb(x)g(x),$$

and g plays the role of y. Equations (6.2) supply the rule

$$\begin{aligned} a(x)p(x)e^{-a(x)g(x)} - rb(x) = 0 \quad &\text{when } g(x) > 0, \\ a(x)p(x) - rb(x) \leq 0 \quad &\text{when } g(x) = 0. \end{aligned} \tag{6.6}$$

If we denote $rb(x)/a(x)$ simply as $c(x)$ then, after a little bit of algebraic juggling, rule (6.6) becomes

$$\begin{aligned} g(x) &= 0 &&\text{if } p(x) \leq c(x), \\ g(x) &= \frac{\ln p(x) - \ln c(x)}{a(x)} &&\text{if } p(x) > c(x), \end{aligned} \tag{6.7}$$

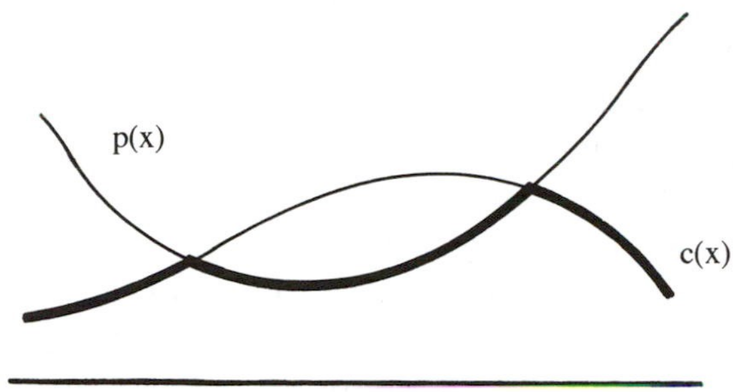

Figure 6.4. The minimum of functions $p(x)$ and $c(x)$ as a dark curve.

where ln is the natural logarithm. This gives the optimal choice of g in terms of a choice of p.

The sub commander wishes to minimize P, or, equivalently, to maximize $1-P$. Now

$$1 - P = \int_R p(x)e^{-a(x)g(x)}\, dx, \tag{6.8}$$

since the integral of $p(x)$ over R is one. (Recall that p is a probability density.) Using the rule (6.7), it is now easy to verify that

$$1 - P \leq \int_R c(x)\, dx, \tag{6.9}$$

and, indeed, if h is a function defined for each x by

$$h(x) = \min\,(p(x), c(x)),$$

then

$$1 - P = \int_R h(x)\, dx \tag{6.10}$$

(Exercise 6.6.2 and Fig. 6.4). It follows that $1 - P$ can never have a value that exceeds the integral over R of either $c(x)$ or $p(x)$, whichever is smaller. The optimum strategy for the submarine, therefore, is now clear. It must choose $p(x)$ so that the area under the curve $h(x)$ is as large as possible. If the integral of the function $c(x)$ over R is less than unity, then it suffices to choose

$p(x)$ everywhere greater than $c(x)$, thereby giving $1 - P$ its largest value, namely, the integral of $c(x)$. On the other hand, if this integral exceeds one, then the optimum is obtained by letting $p(x)$ be everywhere less than $c(x)$, since this gives $1 - P$ a maximum value of one. It follows that no matter how the searcher picks g, the submarine can guarantee a minimum level of detection by properly choosing p.

The functions a and b are determined by external factors and are not at the discretion of either side. Therefore, the value of $c(x)$ is determined solely by the constant r, and the decision as to whether p is less than or greater than c in Eq.(6.7) depends on how small or big r is. Recall that a large r means that the probability of detection is less important than its cost, and conversely, when r is small, detection is paramount over cost.

We can now summarize the optimal tactics of each side in terms of r. When r is small:

$$\begin{aligned} g(x) &= \ln \frac{p(x)/c(x)}{a(x)}, \\ p(x) &= \text{any curve lying below the curve } c(x), \end{aligned}$$

and when r is large:

$$\begin{aligned} g(x) &= 0, \\ p(x) &= \text{any curve lying above the curve } c(x). \end{aligned}$$

Just how small is *small*? The answer is revealed in Exercise 6.6.3.

It is apparent from this discussion that if the cost of search is large enough in certain regions of R, then no effort should be expended there, and that when a search is undertaken it is never proportional to the probability of finding the target. Also note that the optimal tactics for each side of the conflict are chosen on the assumption that the other side can pick its strategy with complete freedom. The pessimistic antagonists believe that the opponent will always choose g or p to thwart the other, and this leads both sides to pick their strategies so as to maximize what they are convinced is their minimum gain.

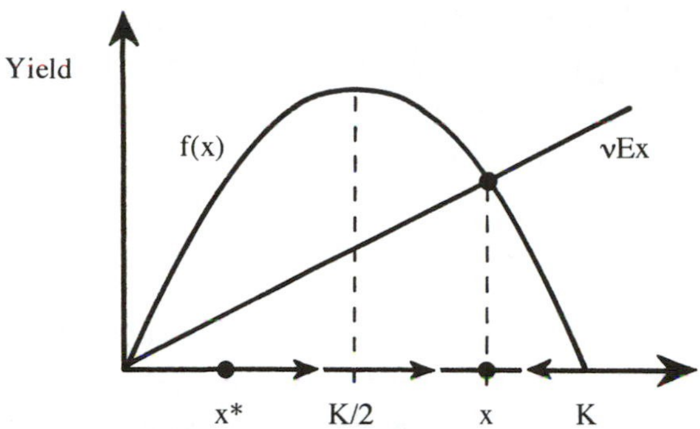

Figure 6.5. A logistic growth law $f(x)$ intersected by the line having slope νE. The point of intersection corresponds to an attractor and the yield from the harvest is the value of f at the attractor.

6.4. A Restricted-Access Fishery

We now return to the fishery model of Section 4.4 and ask some new questions. The fishing grounds provide catches of several species that follow a growth law that we take to be logistic, in place of the form adopted earlier. If, as usual, x denotes the fish density and E the harvesting effort, then x satisfies the differential equation

$$x' = f(x) - \nu E x = rx\left(1 - \frac{x}{K}\right) - \nu E x, \tag{6.11}$$

and the net revenue from the harvest is

$$E(\nu p x - c). \tag{6.12}$$

All terms have the same meaning as before. (We urge the reader to get re-acquainted with Section 4.4 before continuing.)

Equation (6.11) has an equilibrium, for any fixed value of E, obtained by taking the intersection of the curve $f(x) = rx(1 - x/K)$ with the straight line $\nu E x$ (Fig. 6.5). It is an attractor. The total yield is given by the quantity $\nu E x$, and so the maximum yield occurs at $x = K/2$, where $f(x)$ is greatest. However, if the equilibrium is at $x^* = c/\nu p$, and if this is less than $K/2$, as shown in Fig. 6.5, the yield is also less.

In an open-access fishery, each participant hastens to get what he can from the fishery by exploiting it to the utmost, since, as we explained earlier, to do otherwise would mean relinquishing his haul to the other fishermen. Investments in fishing gear and boats are largely irreversible, and so there is every incentive to continue fishing until the net revenue has been driven to zero. Denoting this revenue by $R(E)$, we see from Eq.(6.12) that $R(E) = 0$ precisely at $x = x^*$.

Now consider the opposite situation, in which the fishery has a single owner, a firm or some public entity. In contrast to the remorseless effort exerted in the common access case, a sensible harvesting policy in the absence of competition would be to maximize the revenue R. Instead of trying to bring R down to zero, it might be wiser to restrain the fishing effort so that a positive net income can accrue over some indefinite time horizon. The goal of an individual owner is then to maximize the integral $J(E)$ defined by

$$J(E) = \int_0^\infty e^{-\delta t} R(E(t))\, dt = \int_0^\infty e^{-\delta t} E(\nu p x - c)\, dt \qquad (6.13)$$

by choosing E properly as some function of time t. The factor $e^{-\delta t}$ is introduced to indicate that a future gain is worth less than a current profit by an exponential amount. δ is called a *discount factor.*

The maximum of Eq.(6.13) admits an easy solution. Assume, first, that the fishing effort E is constrained to have a maximum value E_m, corresponding to a limit on fleet size or total gear that can be deployed per unit time: $0 \leq E \leq E_m$. From Eq.(6.11), we see that $E = f(x)/\nu x - x'$ and so Eq.(6.13) may be rewritten as

$$\int_0^\infty e^{-\delta t} \left(p - \frac{c}{\nu x}\right) f(x)\, dt - \int_0^\infty e^{-\delta t} \left(p - \frac{c}{\nu x}\right) x'\, dt. \qquad (6.14)$$

Now define $Z(x)$ by the integral

$$Z(x) = \int_{x^*}^{x} (p - c/\nu u)\, du.$$

Using an integration by parts, the second integral in Eq.(6.14) can be expressed as

$$\int_0^\infty e^{-\delta t} Z(x(t))\, dt + Z(x(0)),$$

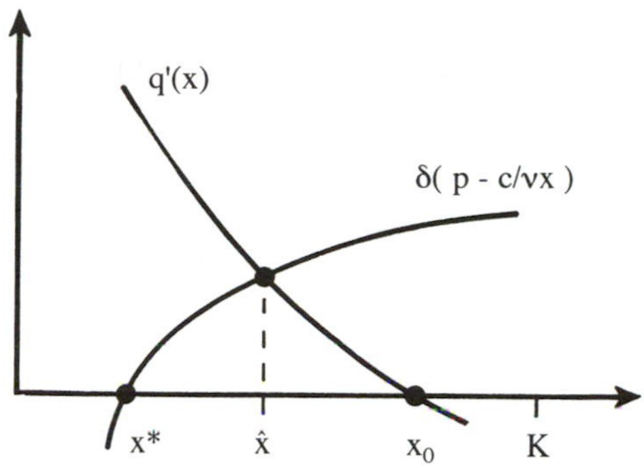

Figure 6.6. Intersection of the curves q' and $\delta(p - c/\nu x)$.

where $x(0)$ is the initial value of x, which we assume to be greater than x^*. As a matter of fact, $x(t)$ will take on values only between K, its maximum population density, and x^*, where the economic incentive to continue fishing is zero.

The expression for $J(E)$ is now

$$J(E) = \int_0^\infty e^{-\delta t} \left(\left(p - \frac{c}{\nu x} \right) f(x) - \delta Z(x) \right) dt. \qquad (6.15)$$

The function $F(x) = (p - c/\nu x) f(x) - \delta Z(x)$ that appears in the integrand has a unique positive maximum $\hat{x}$ somewhere in the interval between x^* and K. To see this, first note that for any given effort E, one has $\nu E x = f(x)$ at an equilibrium x of Eq.(6.11). Therefore, letting $q(x) = f(x)(p - c/\nu x)$, it follows that $q(x) = E(\nu p x - c)$, which is the net revenue associated with the equilibrium value of x. As x increases from x^*, the revenue increases to a maximum at some x_0 and then decreases. It follows that $q'(x)$ is monotone downward, crossing the x axis at x_0. To find the maximum of $F(x)$, we set F' to zero to obtain the equation $q'(x) = \delta(p - c/\nu x)$. The curves q' and $\delta(p - c/\nu x)$ intersect at some $\hat{x}$ that lies between x^* and x_0 (Fig. 6.6).

Note that as δ goes to infinity, $\hat{x}$ tends to x^*. This is what one would expect in view of the fact that $\delta = \infty$ corresponds to completely discounting the future in favor of revenues that are earned immediately. This is the prevalent attitude in a common access fishery, in which, as we have seen, revenue is driven to zero and the biomass level is reduced to x^*.

Since $J(E)$ is to be maximized, it is apparent that $x(t)$ should be chosen so that it reaches $\hat{x}$ from its starting point $x(0)$ as quickly as possible, and then remains there for all subsequent time. This is because $e^{-\delta t}$ is a decreasing function of t, and so it is incumbent to reach the maximum value of $F(x)$ as soon as possible. If x is initially greater (less) than $\hat{x}$, then evidently x' should be chosen to have the largest possible negative (positive) value. It follows that the optimal harvesting policy for a single owner is

$$E(t) = \begin{cases} E_m & \text{if } x(t) > \hat{x}, \\ 0 & \text{if } x(t) < \hat{x}, \\ \dfrac{f(x)}{\nu x} & \text{if } x(t) = \hat{x}. \end{cases} \tag{6.16}$$

Now suppose that the fishery is limited to a finite number of individuals or firms by the imposition of entry fees or licenses, either of which serve to restrict entry. For simplicity, we consider the case of only two owners who vie with each other to exploit the fishery. Each differs in the values of E, p, c, ν; we indicate this by the subscript $i = 1, 2$ to distinguish between them. The basic growth equation (6.11) now becomes

$$x' = f(x) - \nu_1 E_1 x - \nu_2 E_2 x, \tag{6.17}$$

since both owners ply the same waters, and the fish biomass is reduced by their combined efforts. The long-term revenue accrued by each owner is consequently a function of both harvesting rates, and by analogy with Eq.(6.13), we write

$$J_i(E_1, E_2) = \int_0^\infty e^{-\delta_i t}(\nu_i p_i x - c_i) E_i \, dt. \tag{6.18}$$

If each owner works separately, without competition from the other, then each would attain an optimal harvesting level $\hat{x}_i$, $i = 1, 2$, as explained before; but in reality, they must seek a competitive equilibrium that compromises the individual goals of maximizing Eq.(6.18). A pair of $E_i^\#$ will be deemed optimal if

$$\begin{aligned} J_1(E_1^\#, E_2^\#) &\geq J_1(E_1, E_2^\#), \\ J_2(E_1^\#, E_2^\#) &\geq J_2(E_1^\#, E_2), \end{aligned} \tag{6.19}$$

for all admissible E_i that satisfy $0 \le E_i \le \bar{E}_i$. This means that if owner 1, for example, unilaterally changes his strategy while owner 2 sticks to his, then J_1 either remains the same or, at worst, decreases.

Let $x_i^* = c_i/\nu_i p_i$. Then owner 1 is more efficient than owner 2 if $x_1^* < x_2^*$. This means that owner 1 operates at lower costs, or fetches higher prices for his catch, or is technologically better equipped. In this case, the competitive equilibrium is given by the rules

$$E_1^{\#}(t) = \begin{cases} \bar{E}_1 & \text{if } x(t) > \eta, \\ 0 & \text{if } x(t) < \eta, \\ \dfrac{f(x)}{\nu_1 x} & \text{if } x(t) = \eta, \end{cases} \tag{6.20}$$

where $\eta = \min(\hat{x}_1, x_2^*)$, and

$$E_2^{\#}(t) = \begin{cases} \bar{E}_2 & \text{if } x(t) \ge x_2^*, \\ 0 & \text{if } x(t) < x_2^*. \end{cases} \tag{6.21}$$

Let us establish the truth of Eqs.(6.20). The other rule (6.21) is verified in a similar fashion (Exercise 6.6.5). To begin, define $f_1(x)$ by

$$f_1(x) = \begin{cases} f(x) - \nu_2 E_2 x & \text{if } x \ge x_2^*, \\ f(x) & \text{if } x < x_2^*. \end{cases}$$

If $\bar{E}_2$ is large enough, f_1 is negative for $x \ge x_2^*$. Now assume that rule (6.21) holds. Then Eq.(6.17) becomes

$$x' = f_1(x) - \nu_1 E_1 x.$$

By analogy with the way $F(x)$ was defined before, let

$$F_1(x) = \left(p_1 - \frac{c_1}{\nu_1 x}\right) f_1(x) - Z_1(x),$$

in which Z_1 is the same integral as Z except that its lower limit is x_1^*. It is always true that $\hat{x}_1 > x_1^*$. Moreover, since $x_1^* < x_2^*$ then Fig. (6.7) shows that F_1 is maximized by choosing x equal to the smallest of $\hat{x}_1$ and x_2^* because $F_1(x)$ is immediately negative as soon as x exceeds x_2^*. The form of F_1 in this figure is arrived at from the same considerations that applied to F earlier. We conclude that

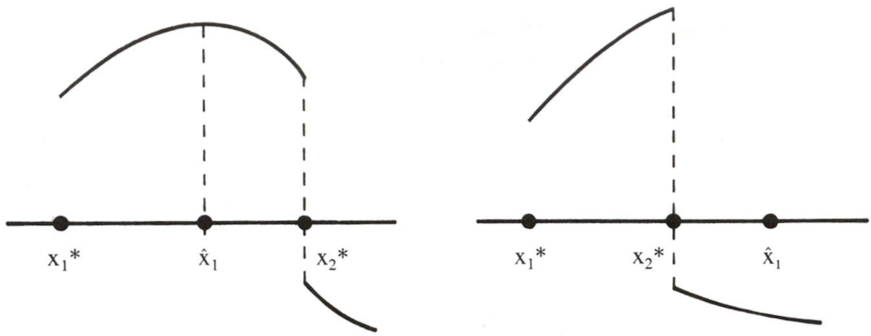

Figure 6.7. Maxima of the function f_1 in two cases.

$J_1(E_1, E_2^{\#})$ must be maximized by rule (6.20), for the reason that $J(E)$ for a single owner was maximized previously using Eqs.(6.16). The interpretation of this result is that if owner 1 is more efficient, then he drives owner 2 out of business, since x is quickly brought down to a value at which the net revenue to 2 is zero. Since $\eta > x_1^*$, the revenue garnered by owner 1 is positive. When $\hat{x}_1 > x_2^*$, owner 1 eliminates his competitor by fishing more intensely than if this inequality is reversed. In effect, the first owner must work hard to keep his competitor from returning. Finally, in the case in which $x_1^* = x_2^*$, the revenues of both parties are evidently dissipated to zero and the situation is no better than in an open-access fishery.

In summary, we see that if the goal of limited access is to safeguard against overfishing, it is not a very successful ploy, since the intense competition between participants insures that the fish stocks will be reduced as far as necessary to achieve the complete elimination of those who are less efficient. This may be recognized as another form of the principle of competitive exclusion that we encountered in Chapter 4. Evidently, some other form of control, such as catch quotas or a tax on the harvest, is required for effective conservation.

6.5. A Commentary

It is interesting to compare the optimal strategies adopted by the various participants in the two previous sections. We have no intention of delving into the formalism of game theory, where these matters are discussed in more detail, but only wish to comment, in a slightly more abstract way, on the different approaches that were used.

There are two competitors $C_i, i = 1, 2$, who aim to achieve certain goals, but each is constrained by the presence of the other. The naval officers of the opposing forces, for example, have the goals of evading detection in order to launch torpedoes, on one side, and of locating the submarine and preventing it from completing its mission, on the other.

Let $G_1(u, v)$ and $G_2(u, v)$ represent the gain to each side, where u and v are strategies that are available to C_1 and C_2, respectively. In the submarine problem, C_i are measures of detection and evasion, as you recall, and u, v describe how searcher and target place themselves in the ocean.

If C_1 is pessimistic, as in the submarine problem, he believes that C_2 will try to thwart him by choosing a strategy v that will minimize G_1. Therefore, C_1 adopts a conservative attitude and picks u to maximize his minimum gain. The other competitor, equally suspicious, behaves similarly. Letting u_0, v_0 be a pair of optimal strategies for each side, this means that

$$\begin{aligned} G_1(u_0, v_0) &\leq G_1(u_0, v), \\ G_2(u_0, v_0) &\leq G_2(u, v_0). \end{aligned} \tag{6.22}$$

The first inequality expresses the idea that no matter what v is picked by C_2, the gain to C_1 can never be less than $G_1(u_0, v_0)$ as long as C_1 chooses u_0. The second inequality has a similar interpretation. This is known as a *maxmin equilibrium*, as it appeared in Section 6.3.

What is being ignored here, of course, is the question as to whether optimal strategies exist to begin with, a mathematical issue that belongs to the domain of game theory.

A different competitive approach is the one adopted by the two owners of a fishery, in which both sides select strategies u_0, v_0 so that any unilateral change on the part of C_1, for example, to some other u can only decrease G_1, as long as C_2 sticks to using v_0. This may be expressed as a pair of inequalities:

$$\begin{aligned} G_1(u_0, v_0) &\geq G_1(u, v_0), \\ G_2(u_0, v_0) &\geq G_2(u_0, v). \end{aligned} \tag{6.23}$$

This is referred to as a *competitive equilibrium.*

A comparison of these approaches shows that maxmin and competitive equilibria need not equal each other, since one is based on pessimism and the other on greed. There is one situation in which the two approaches are equal, however. Suppose that $G_1(u, v) = -G_2(u, v)$ so that a gain to one side is a loss to the other, as would be the case, for example, if the parameter r in the submarine problem is set to zero. Then Eqs.(6.22) and (6.23) reduce to the same strategy pair (Exercise 6.6.1).

Although it plays no role in the models discussed in this chapter, there is yet another form of equilibrium in which the two players decide to cooperate by helping one another up to the point of disadvantage to themselves. In this way, it is conceivable that the optimal return to each could be greater than if they opted for a noncooperative equilibrium. A cooperative equilibrium can be defined as a pair u_0, v_0 for which there is no other u, v for which

$$\begin{aligned} G_1(u_0, v_0) &\leq G_1(u, v), \\ G_2(u_0, v_0) &\leq G_2(u, v), \end{aligned}$$

with at least one of these inequalities being strict. What this means is that any move away from an optimal pair of strategies can only make one of the players worse off.

6.6. Exercises

6.6.1. Use inequalities (6.22) and (6.23) to show that they lead to the same optimal strategies in the case in which $G_1(u, v) + G_2(u, v) = 0$, the so-called *zero-sum situation.*

6.6.2. Establish the identity (6.10).

6.6.3. In the statement of an optimal strategy for the two naval opponents in Section 6.3, we distinguished between *small* and *large* r. Show that the difference between small and large occurs at the critical value

$$r = \frac{1}{\displaystyle\int_R \frac{b(x)}{a(x)}\,dx}.$$

6.6.4. A submarine wishes to pass through a channel of length L undetected by an airplane that patrols back and forth across the channel. This is called a *barrier patrol*, since the path of the plane is perpendicular to that of the boat. The sub cannot be detected when submerged, but it can only remain under the water for a maximum distance of $d < L$. The channel has a varying width, and if the plane patrols the widest part, it cannot do so as efficiently as when it patrols the narrower parts. Nevertheless, the plane varies the position of the patrol at random every day to avoid giving the submarine commander the knowledge he needs to dive under the barrier and elude detection. The probability density of the positions where the patrol takes place is given by $g(x)$. The integral of g over the length of the channel is one.

The situation is illustrated in Fig. 6.8. If the patrol is at position x and the boat attempts to go by on the surface, then the conditional probability of detection is $p(x)$, where p is smaller where the channel is wide and larger where the channel is narrow.

Let $h(x)$ denote the probability that the sub is submerged at position x. A little thought will convince one that the integral of h over the length of the channel is d. We allow the sub to submerge for a distance less than d and then re-submerge elsewhere, as it chooses, provided

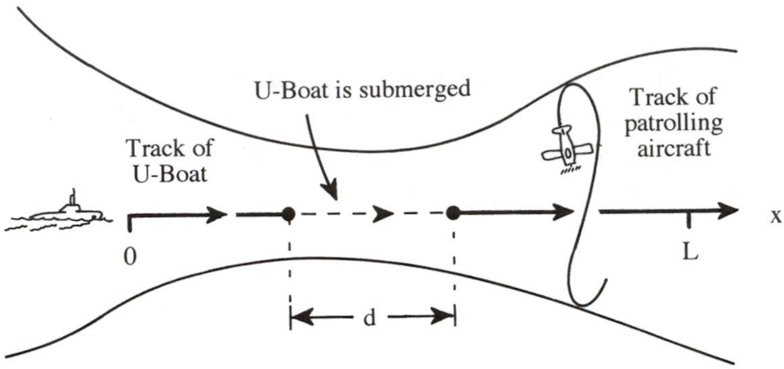

Figure 6.8. A barrier patrol in a channel of length L and varying width.

that the total distance sums to d. The plane wishes to choose the function g to maximize the probability of detection, no matter what the sub does (a maxmin strategy), while the sub wants to maximize the probability of not being detected, regardless of what the plane does, by picking the function h. This, too, is a maxmin strategy. Formulate this problem mathematically and make an attempt at a solution.

6.6.5. Establish rule (6.21) by assuming that Eqs.(6.20) hold and then showing that $J_2(E_1^{\#}, E_2)$ is maximized by (6.21).

6.6.6. A version of the model in Section 6.3 can be formulated as an optimization problem that is reminiscent of the type considered in Chapters 2 and 3. Suppose that the region R of the ocean is partitioned into N subsets, and that the probability the submarine is within the ith subset is a fixed number $p_i, i = 1, 2 \ldots N$, where the p_i sum to unity. An amount of search effort g_i is allocated to region i, in terms of fuel, aircraft, time, or some other limited resource. The sum of the g_i is some stipulated constant that represents the total amount of available resources that can be expended in the search. The conditional probability of a sighting in region i, given that the target is actually within this area, is $1 - e^{-a_i g_i}$, where a_i is the visibility factor in area i. (Recall the discussion in Section 6.3.) The goal is to maximize the probability of detection within R by choosing the deployments g_i optimally. Formulate this problem mathematically.

6.6.7. Another application of search theory arises in police work. Suppose that a police vehicle is assigned a sector or *beat* in which there are c street miles that are accessible to patrol and that the average speed is v miles per hour. In time t, the vehicle moves a distance vt at random. This means that the movement is generally zigzag through the streets to reduce any element of predictability on the part of a criminal. For small enough t, it is unlikely that the patrol car will overlap the path it just covered, however. The small distance vt is randomly located among the c miles of street network, and a crime incident is also assumed to be located at random within the same c miles (thefts, muggings, and the like). Therefore the probability that in time t, the path of the random patrol overlaps the location of a crime in progress is simply vt/c. This is the conditional probability of detecting a crime, given that there is a crime in progress during time t. As t increases, so does the likelihood that the patrol car will retrace part of its own path, and so this simple ratio is no longer an accurate description of the detection probability. However, one can reason as follows. Let $P(t)$ be the probability of no detection during t. Increase t by a small increment Δt. Non-overlapping time intervals are assumed to give independent events, and so it follows that $P(t + \Delta t) = P(t)P(\Delta t)$. However, $P(\Delta t) = 1 - (v\Delta t/c)$ and by letting Δt go to zero one shows that P satisfies the differential equation $P' = -(v/c)P$. Verify this and establish that the conditional probability of detecting a crime in progress during any time t is $1 - e^{-vt/c}$. This is similar to the law of diminishing returns that we encountered in the search for submarines in Section 6.3.

6.7. Further Readings

Although the models in this chapter are faintly contrived and less convincing than the ones that were considered previously, it is nevertheless true that they reflect real issues. The hide-and-seek game, for example, was played out many times during the Second World War, and in the annals of the military operations of that time there are tales reminiscent of the one we looked at (see, for example, the book by Waddington [37]), and the restricted-access fishery issue has been confronted by several nations.

Our discussion of the limited-entry fishery is based on the paper by Clark [38], while the search problem is adapted from [39]. The topic of search theory has wider applicability than just hunting for submarines and has been applied to police patrols ([40] and Exercise 6.6.7) and a variety of Navy and Coast Guard search missions.

A

Conditional Probability and Conditional Expectation

A few facts concerning probability that are needed in Chapter 3 are reviewed here. For further details, consult the first three chapters of the book *Introduction To Probability Models* by S. Ross [13].

Let A and B denote events in a sample space S. The *conditional probability* of A given B, written $\text{prob}\,(A|B)$ is defined by

$$\text{prob}\,(A|B)\,\text{prob}\,(B) = \text{prob}\,(AB) \tag{A.1}$$

where AB is the joint event of A and B. When $\text{prob}\,(A|B) = \text{prob}\,(A)$, we say that A and B are independent.

As an example, suppose that X and Y are discrete random variables taking on the values $0, 1, 2, \ldots$ If A is the event "$X = k$" and B is "$Y = i$", then the probability of the joint event AB is written as $\text{prob}\,(X = k, Y = i)$, and Eq.(A.1) is then

$$\text{prob}\,(X = k|Y = i)\,\text{prob}\,(Y = i) = \text{prob}\,(X = k, Y = i).$$

Let B_i be a collection of disjoint events indexed by $i = 0, 1, 2\ldots,$

whose union is S. Then

$$\text{prob}\,(A) = \sum_{i=0}^{\infty} \text{prob}\,(AB_i). \tag{A.2}$$

In terms of the random variables X and Y, this means that

$$\text{prob}\,(X = k) = \sum_{i=0}^{\infty} \text{prob}\,(X = k, Y = i).$$

By virtue of Eq.(A.1), one can write Eq.(A.2) as

$$\text{prob}\,(A) = \sum_{i=0}^{\infty} \text{prob}\,(A|B_i)\,\text{prob}\,(B_i), \tag{A.3}$$

and so, for the variables X and Y, one has

$$\text{prob}\,(X = k) = \sum_{i=0}^{\infty} \text{prob}\,(X = k|Y = i)\,\text{prob}\,(Y = i).$$

The *expected value* (also called the *mean value*) of X is defined by

$$E(X) = \sum_{k=0}^{\infty} k\text{prob}\,(X = k),$$

and if $h(X)$ is some function of X, then the expected value of the random variable $h(X)$ is given by

$$E(h(X)) = \sum_{k=0}^{\infty} h(k)\text{prob}\,(X = k). \tag{A.4}$$

For example, if $h(X) = X^2$, then

$$E(X^2) = \sum_{k=0}^{\infty} k^2\text{prob}\,(X = k).$$

The *conditional expectation (conditional mean)* of X, given that $Y = i$, is defined by

$$E(X|Y = i) = \sum_{k=0}^{\infty} k\text{prob}\,(X = k|Y = i). \tag{A.5}$$

This allows us to define $E(X|Y)$ as a function of Y; call it $h(Y)$, whose value, when $Y = i$, is given by Eq.(A.5). From Eqs.(A.4) and (A.3), one therefore obtains the unconditional expectation of X as

$$\begin{aligned} E(E(X|Y) &= \sum_{i=0}^{\infty} h(i)\text{prob}\,(Y=i) = \sum_{i=0}^{\infty} E(X|Y=i)\text{prob}\,(Y=i) \\ &= \sum_{i=0}^{\infty}\sum_{k=0}^{\infty} k\text{prob}\,(x=k|Y=i)\,\text{prob}\,(y=i) \\ &= \sum_{k=0}^{\infty} k \sum_{i=0}^{\infty} \text{prob}\,(x=k, Y=i) = \sum_{k=0}^{\infty} k\text{prob}\,(X=k). \end{aligned}$$

It follows that

$$E(X) = E(E(X|Y). \tag{A.6}$$

When X and Y are continuous random variables taking on nonnegative real values, the discrete set of events indexed by $0, 1, \ldots$ is replaced by a continuum of events indexed by the nonnegative real numbers s, and the sum is replaced by an integral. In addition, the discrete probabilities prob $(X = k)$ are now represented by a continuous density function $f(s)$. For example, if X and Y are exponentially distributed random variables (see Section 3.2 for a definition), in which the density of Y is $f(s) = \mu e^{-\mu s}$, for $s \geq 0$, with $f(s) = 0$ for $s < 0$, consider the event "$X < Y$," which means that the value assumed by X is less than the values assumed by Y. Equations (A.2) amd (A.3) now become

$$\text{prob}\,(X < Y) = \int_0^{\infty} \text{prob}\,(X < Y, Y = s)\,ds$$

and

$$\text{prob}\,(X < Y) = \int_0^{\infty} \text{prob}\,(X < Y|Y = s)\mu e^{-\mu s}\,ds. \tag{A.7}$$

Finally, Eq.(A.6) continues to be true and is expressed as

$$E(X) = E(E(X|Y)) = \int_0^{\infty} E(X|Y = s)\mu e^{-\mu s}\,ds.$$

For example, suppose that Z is a random variable defined by $Z = 1$ if "$X < Y$" and $Z = 0$ otherwise. Then $E(Z) = \text{prob}\,(Z = 1) = \text{prob}\,(X < Y)$ and $E(Z|Y = s) = \text{prob}\,(X < Y|Y = s)$, and it therefore follows from Eq.(A.6) that Eq.(A.7) must be true.

B

Linear Second-Order Differential Equations

Reference is occasionally made in the text to equations of the form

$$x'' + ax' + bx = 0, \tag{B.1}$$

where a and b are real constants. Using the procedure adopted in Section 4.2, this second-order equation may be rewritten as a pair of first-order equations by letting $x_1 = x$ and $x_2 = x'$. In terms of the new variables, we get

$$\begin{aligned} x_1' &= x_2 \\ x_2' &= -bx_1 - ax_2 \end{aligned} \tag{B.2}$$

or, in vector notation,

$$\begin{pmatrix} x_1' \\ x_2' \end{pmatrix} = \begin{pmatrix} 0 & 1 \\ -b & -a \end{pmatrix} \begin{pmatrix} x_1 \\ x_2 \end{pmatrix}. \tag{B.3}$$

By direct substitution into Eq.(B.1), it is easy to verify that $e^{\lambda t}$ is a solution, provided that λ satisfies the quadratic equation

$$\lambda^2 + a\lambda + b = 0.$$

The two solutions to this quadratic, which we assume here to be distinct for simplicity, are given by

$$\lambda = -\frac{a}{2} \pm \frac{(a^2 - 4b)^{1/2}}{2} \tag{B.4}$$

These roots are recognized as the eigenvalues of the matrix in Eq.(B.3).

Writing the distict eigenvalues as λ_1 and λ_2, it is now simple to check that any linear combination of $e^{-\lambda_1 t}$ is also a solution to Eq.(B.1):

$$x(t) = c_1 e^{-\lambda_1 t} + c_2 e^{-\lambda_2 t} \tag{B.5}$$

for real scalars $c_i, i = 1, 2$. These scalars can be chosen to satisfy specific initial values of $x(0)$ and $x'(0)$. Consider, for example, the equation $x'' - 4x = 0$, in which we are given the initial conditions $x(0) = 4$ and $x'(0) = 2$. Then one readily computes the λ_i to be $2, -2$, respectively, and so Eq.(B.5) gives

$$x(t) = c_1 e^{2t} + c_2 e^{-2t}.$$

Differentiating, we find that

$$x'(t) = 2c_1 e^{2t} - 2c_2 e^{-2t}.$$

When $t = 0$, we obtain $4 = c_1$ and $2 = 2c_1 - 2c_2 = 8 - 2c_2$. Therefore,

$$x(t) = 4e^{2t} + 3e^{-2t}.$$

When $a^2 - 4b$ is negative, the eigenvalues are complex numbers, with λ_1 the complex conjugate of λ_2. For notational reasons, let us write $\lambda_1 = -a/2 + i(4b - a^2)^{1/2}/2$ as $q + iw$. By DeMoivre's formula, we recall that $e^{(q+iw)t} = e^{qt}e^{iwt} = e^{qt}(\cos wt + i \sin wt)$. It is simple to verify that the real and imaginary parts of this expression are each solutions of Eq.(B.1) and, therefore, so is any linear combination of these parts. Thus, when the roots are complex, we obtain

$$x(t) = e^{qt}(c_1 \cos wt + c_2 \sin wt). \tag{B.6}$$

For an example of Eq.(B.6), consider the equation $x'' + 4x' + 13x = 0$, with initial conditions $x(0) = 2$ and $x'(0) = 0$. The eigenvalues in this case are $-2 + i3$ and $-2 - i3$. From Eq.(B.6), we obtain

$$x(t) = e^{-2t}(c_1 \cos 3t + c_2 \sin 3t),$$

and the derivative is computed as

$$x'(t) = 3e^{-2t}(-c_1 \sin 3t + c_2 \cos 3t).$$

When $t = 0$, one finds that $2 = c_1$ and $0 = 3c_2$, and the solution is therefore

$$x(t) = 2e^{-2t} \cos 3t.$$

For more details on second-order equations, see Chapter 6 of the book *Differential Equations* by Redheffer [25].

C

Vector Functions

In this appendix, we summarize a few facts concerning smooth vector-valued functions $\mathbf{u}(t)$ of a variable t, where $\mathbf{u}$ is defined by

$$\mathbf{u}(t) = \begin{pmatrix} u_1(t) \\ \vdots \\ u_n(t) \end{pmatrix}.$$

The scalar-valued real functions have continous derivatives in t. The derivative of $\mathbf{u}$ is denoted by

$$\mathbf{u}'(t) = \begin{pmatrix} u_1'(t) \\ \vdots \\ u_n'(t) \end{pmatrix}.$$

If we are given two such functions $\mathbf{u}$ and $\mathbf{v}$, their inner product is defined for all t by the scalar function

$$\mathbf{u}^T(t)\mathbf{v}(t) = \sum_{i=1}^{n} u_i(t)v_i(t).$$

In particular, the length of $\mathbf{u}$ is given in terms of the inner product as $||\mathbf{u}(t)|| = \mathbf{u}^T(t)\mathbf{u}(t)$. If $\mathbf{u}$ and $\mathbf{v}$ have a zero inner product, we say that they are orthogonal.

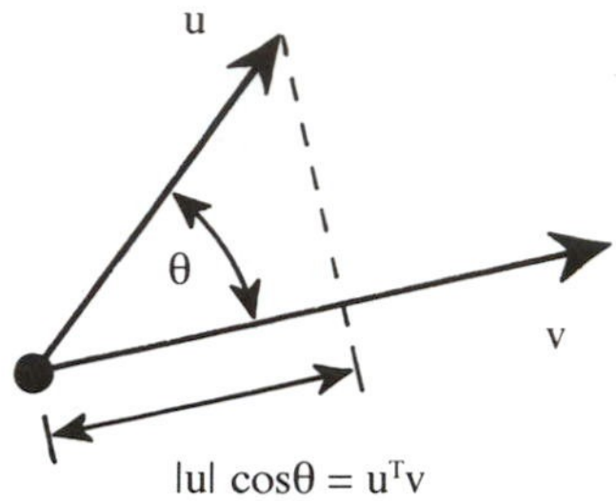

Figure C.1. The component of **u** in the direction of **v** is the projection of **u** onto **v**.

In the special case of two-dimensional vectors in the plane, the cosine of the angle Θ between them is shown in calculus texts to be defined in terms of the inner product as $\cos\Theta = \mathbf{u}^T\mathbf{v}/||\mathbf{u}||\,||\mathbf{v}||$. Clearly, the cosine is zero when **u** and **v** are orthogonal, namely, when **u** is perpendicular to **v**. If the length of **v** is one, then the component of **u** in the direction of **v** is easily seen to equal $\mathbf{u}^T\mathbf{v}$ (Fig. C.1).

Let us consider some examples of vector functions in the plane. If C is a smooth curve, it is defined parametrically in terms of its coordinates x and y by the position vector $\mathbf{r}(t) = (x(t), y(t))$, where t is a real parameter. As t varies, $\mathbf{r}(t)$ traces out the curve C in the direction of increasing t. An example is the unit circle defined by $\mathbf{r}(t) = (\cos\Theta t, \sin\Theta t)$, which is traced out in a counterclockwise fashion. Since $\mathbf{r}$ is written as a row vector, it coincides with our previous notation if we let $\mathbf{u} = \mathbf{r}^T$, where superscript T denotes vector transpose. Also, in this case, $u_1 = x$ and $u_2 = y$.

In calculus texts, it is shown that the derivative $\mathbf{r}'(t) = (x'(t), y'(t))$ is tangent to the curve C at the point defined by the position $\mathbf{r}(t)$. If $\mathbf{n}$ is a vector orthogonal to $\mathbf{r}'$ at any t, we say that $\mathbf{n}$ is normal to C at that point (Fig. C.2). The region to the left (right) of C as t increases may be called the interior (exterior) of C. If the normal points inward, it is called an *inner normal*; otherwise, it is an *outer normal.*

For another example, consider a system of first-order differential equations $\mathbf{p}' = f(p)$, where $\mathbf{p}(t)$ is a smooth vector with components

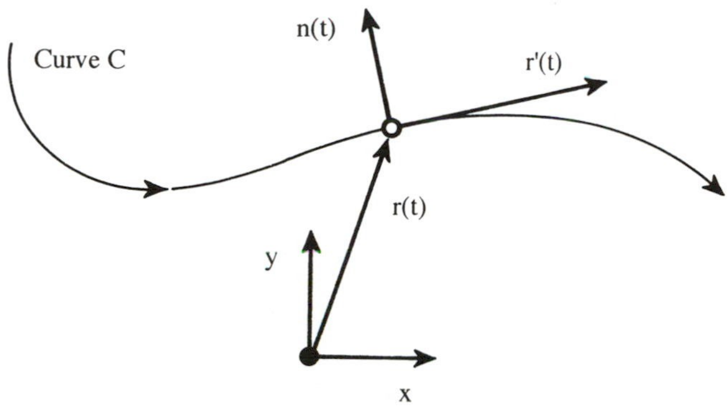

Figure C.2. A curve C in the plane with position vector $\mathbf{r}$, tangent $\mathbf{r}'$, and normal $\mathbf{n}$.

$p_i(t)$. The vector $\mathbf{p}'$ points in the direction of the flow of the solution trajectory $\mathbf{p}$, for all t. If the solution crosses a curve C defined parametrically as before, then it points to the inside of C at the point of crossing if the cosine of the angle it makes with the inner normal is positive.

Bibliography

[1] White, H.C. *Chains of Opportunity: System Models of Mobility in Organizations.* Harvard Press, 1970.

[2] Chase, I. "Vacancy Chains," *Annual Review of Sociology* **17**,1991, 133-154.

[3] Weissburg, M., L.Roseman, and I. Chase. "Chains of Opportunity: A Markov Model for the Acquisition of Reusable Resources," *Evolutionary Biology* **5**, 1991, 105-117.

[4] Maltz, M. *Recidivism.* Academic Press, 1984.

[5] Blumstein, A., and R. Larson. "Problems in Modeling and Measuring Recidivism," *J. of Research in Crime and Delinquency*, 1971, 124-132.

[6] Kemeny, J., and L. Snell. *Finite Markov Chains.* D. Van Nostrand, 1960.

[7] Kemeny, J., and L. Snell. *Mathematical Models in the Social Sciences.* Ginn, 1961.

[8] Mechling, J. "A Successful Innovation: Manpower Scheduling," *J. of Urban Analysis*, 1974, 259–313.

[9] Bodin, L. "Towards A General Model for Manpower Scheduling, Parts 1 and 2," *J. of Urban Analysis*, 1973, 191–208 and 223–246.

[10] Balinski, M., and P. Young. *Fair Representation.* Yale University Press, 1982.

[11] Beltrami, E., and L. Bodin. "Networks and Vehicle Routing for Municipal Waste Collection," *Networks* **4**, 1974, 65–94.

[12] Tucker, A. "Perfect Graphs and an Application to Optimizing Municipal Services," *SIAM Rev.* **15**, 1973, 585–590.

[13] Ross, S. *Introduction To Probability Models.* Academic Press, Boston, 1990.

[14] Kolesar,P., and E. Blum. "Square Root Laws for Fire Engine Response Distances," *Management Science* **19**, 1973, 1368–1378.

[15] Walker, W., J. Chaiken, and E. Ignall, eds. *Fire Department Deployment Analysis*, Elsevier North-Holland, 1979.

[16] Carter,G., J. Chaiken, and E. Ignall. "Response Areas For Two Emergency Units," *Operations Research* **20**, 1972, 571–594.

[17] Kolesar, P., and W. Walker. "An Algorithm for the Dynamic Relocation of Fire Companies," *Operations Research* **22**, 1974, 249–274.

[18] Frauenthal, J. *Smallpox.* Birkhauser, 1981.

[19] Clark, C. *Mathematical Bioeconomics.* John Wiley, 1976.

[20] Bailey, N. *The Mathematical Theory of Infectious Diseases.* Charles Griffin, 1975.

[21] Aumann, R., and M. Maschler, "Game Theoretic Analysis of a Bankruptcy Problem in the Talmud," *Journal of Economic Theory* **36**, 1985, 195–213.

[22] Braun, M., C. Coleman, and D. Drew, eds. *Differential Equation Models.* Springer-Verlag, 1983.

[23] Arrow, K., and L. Hurwicz. "On The Stability Of The Competitive Equilibrium I and II," *Econometrica* **26**, 1958, 522–552, and *Econometrica* **27**, 1959, 82–109.

[24] Tuchinsky, P. *Man in Competition with the Spruce Budworm.* Birkhauser, 1981.

[25] Redheffer, R. *Differential Equations.* Jones and Bartlett, 1991.

[26] Olsen, L.F., and W.M. Schaeffer. "Chaos Versus Noisy Periodicity: Alternative Hypothesis for Childhood Epidemics," *Science* **249**,1990, 499–504.

[27] Pool, R. "Is It Chaos Or Is It Just Noise?," *Science* **243**, 1989, 25–28.

[28] Crutchfield, J., J. Farmer, N. Packard, and R. Shaw, "Chaos," *Scientific American*, December, 1986.

[29] Hardin, G. "The Tragedy Of The Commons," *Science* **162**, 1968, 1243–1248.

[30] Ermentrout, B. *Phaseplane, Version 3.0.* Brooks/Cole, 1990.

[31] Kocak, H. *Differential and Difference Equations through Computer Experiments, Second Edition.* Springer-Verlag, 1989.

[32] Slobodkin, L., and H. Kierstead, "The Size of Water Masses Containing Plankton Blooms," *J. of Marine Research* **12**, 1953, 141–147.

[33] Okubo, A., P.K. Maini, M.H. Williamson, and J.D Murray, "On the Spatial Spread of the Grey Squirrel in Britain," *Proc. Royal Soc. Lond. B* **238**, 1989, 113–125.

[34] Okubo, A. *Diffusion and Ecological Problems.* Springer-Verlag, 1980.

[35] Murray, J.D. *Mathematical Biology.* Springer-Verlag, 1989.

[36] Weyl, P. "Pollution Susceptibility: An Environmental Parameter for Coastal Zone Management," *Coastal Zone Management Journal* **2**, 1976, 327–343.

[37] Waddington, C.H. *OR in World War II: Operations Research Against The U-boat.* Elek, London, 1973.

[38] Clark, C. "Restricted Access to Common-Property Fishery Resources: A Game-Theoretic Analysis," *Dynamic Optimization and Mathematical Economics.* Plenum Publishing, 1980, 117–132.

[39] Koopman, B.O. *Search and Screening.* Pergamon Press, 1980.

[40] Chelst, K. "The Basics of Search Theory Applied to Police Patrols," in *Police Deployment* (R. Larson, ed.). D.C.Heath, 1978, 161–182.

Index